USBORNE WORLD HISTORY
MEDIEVAL WORLD

Jane Bingham

Designed by Susie McCaffrey, Melissa Alaverdy, Linda Penny and Robin Farrow

History consultant: Dr. Anne Millard

Illustrated by Inklink Firenze,
Giacinto Gaudenzi, Nicholas Hewetson, Lorenzo Cecchi,
Ian Jackson, Justine Torode and David Cuzik

Map illustrations by Jeremy Gower

Additional illustrations by Gerald Wood, Jeremy Gower, Peter Dennis, Stephen Conlin,
Ross Watton, Richard Draper, Simon Roulstone, John Fox, Joseph McEwan,
Cecco Mariniello, Sue Stitt and Jason Lewis

Edited by Fiona Chandler
Artwork co-ordinator: Cathy Lowe
Managing editor: Jane Chisholm   Managing designer: Mary Cartwright

Contents

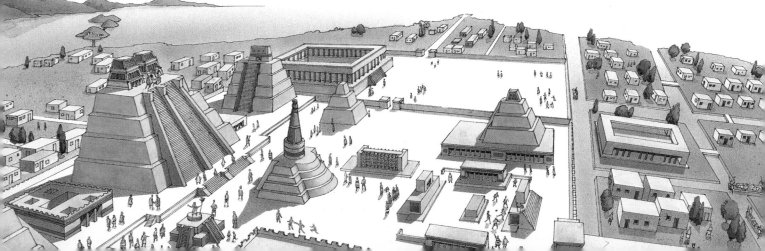

When? Where? How?

Medieval craftworkers

This book describes what was happening all over the world from around the year 500 until around 1500. This time in history is called the medieval period. It is also known as the Middle Ages.

When did it happen?

To help you see which part of the Middle Ages you are reading about, there is a timeline running across the bottom of each double page.

Important events and their dates are shown in boxes. If a date has a letter "c." in front of it, this means that experts are not sure exactly when the event took place. The "c." stands for *circa* which means "about" in Latin.

Sometimes, centuries are mentioned. The 6th century covers all the dates in the 500s, the 7th century covers all the dates in the 600s, and so on.

Where did it happen?

There are maps throughout the book to show you exactly where things happened. You can also check which area of the world you are reading about by looking at the bottom corner of each page. The different areas of the world are marked on the map below.

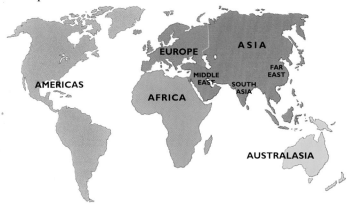

How do we know?

The people of the Middle Ages have left behind lots of evidence about their way of life.

Many buildings and objects survive from medieval times. By studying the places where people lived and the things that they owned, it is possible to build up a vivid picture of life in the Middle Ages.

The Cathedral of the Annunciation, a medieval building in Moscow

Stained-glass portrait of an English lord

Medieval paintings and carvings, mosaics, tapestries and stained-glass windows often show important people and events. They also reveal many fascinating details about everyday life.

In many parts of the medieval world, people wrote things down in handwritten books, called manuscripts. Some writers kept records of important events, while others wrote stories based on real life. Explorers described their travels, inventors explained their ideas, and merchants kept notes about goods that they bought and sold.

The Byzantine Empire

By the year 400, the Roman Empire had split into two parts. The Empire in the west was attacked by warlike tribes and collapsed in 476, but the Empire in the east survived for another thousand years. The eastern Empire was known as the Byzantine Empire because its capital city, Constantinople, was originally called Byzantium.

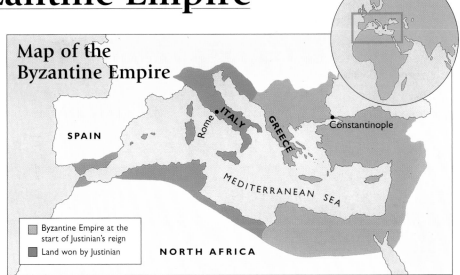

Map of the Byzantine Empire

SPAIN

Rome • ITALY

GREECE

Constantinople

MEDITERRANEAN SEA

NORTH AFRICA

Byzantine Empire at the start of Justinian's reign

Land won by Justinian

Mosaic of the Byzantine Emperor Justinian

Justinian's Empire

In the 6th century, the Byzantine Emperor Justinian won back many of the lands that had once been part of the Roman Empire. Under him, the Byzantine Empire was larger than it would ever be again.

Justinian's palace in Constantinople

Running the Empire

Justinian's dream was to create a great Christian empire. With the help of his wife, Theodora, he set up a new system of laws, and gave orders for many churches to be built. Priests, artists and merchants all visited his palace.

Canal

Emperor Justinian

Empress Theodora

Priest

Court lady

Merchants from North Africa visit Justinian's court.

Visitors grovel in front of the emperor.

Palace guard

EUROPE

500   600   700   800   900

Byzantine art

Byzantine artists were famous for their delicate embroidery and ivory carvings. They also created huge, glittering mosaics and painted dramatic religious portraits, called icons.

Silk embroidery

An icon of the Virgin Mary and Child

Defending the Empire

The Byzantines fought constant battles against Muslim Arabs and Turks. They were threatened by tribes from the north, and even had to fight against Crusaders from western Europe, who were supposed to be on their side (see page 43).

The end of the Empire

After Justinian's death, the Empire became smaller and smaller, and by 1400 only the land around Constantinople was left. In 1453, an army of Ottoman Turks attacked the city. After six weeks of fighting, the Byzantines surrendered and their Empire collapsed.

This picture shows the Ottomans' final attack on Constantinople.

The Byzantine soldiers are weak and exhausted.

Religious split

Christians in the Byzantine Empire developed their own style of church building and held services in Greek, instead of Latin. The Byzantine Church was led by the Patriarch in Constantinople.

Justinian built the Cathedral of Saint Sophia in Constantinople. (It was later turned into a mosque.)

After many quarrels between the Patriarch and the Pope (the head of the Church in the west), the Byzantine Church split away from the Church in the west.

The Ottoman troops have powerful cannons.

Important dates

395	The Roman Empire is divided in two.
476	The Roman Empire in the west collapses.
527-565	Justinian reigns as Byzantine Emperor.
1054	The eastern Church splits from the western Church.
1204	Crusaders capture Constantinople.
1261	The Byzantines drive out the Crusaders.
1453	The Ottoman Turks conquer Constantinople.

EUROPE

The Barbarian Kingdoms

The Romans first used the name "barbarian" to describe the tribes of warriors who invaded their Empire from the northeast. The barbarians swept across Europe destroying the Roman Empire, but, by around 500, they had begun to settle down in their own independent kingdoms.

Map of the main barbarian kingdoms

IRELAND

Barbarian brooch

Canterbury

• Paris

ATLANTIC OCEAN

Constantinople

Rome

MEDITERRANEAN SEA

AFRICA

- Angles and Saxons
- Franks
- Ostrogoths
- Vandals
- Visigoths

A barbarian invader

Barbarian villages

The barbarians wanted to be rich like the Romans, but in fact they destroyed the Roman way of life. Most barbarians lived in small farming villages and let the Roman cities fall into ruins.

The kingdom of the Franks

The largest barbarian kingdom was created by Clovis, leader of the Franks. He made his capital in Paris and started a line of kings. The Frankish kingdom lasted for 300 years and was inherited by Charlemagne (see page 18).

Clovis and his queen Clothilda, painted by a later artist

Barbarian treasures

Some of the barbarians were very skilled at metalwork. They made elaborate swords and drinking cups, as well as beautiful crowns and brooches for their kings and chiefs.

Visigoth crown

A barbarian village

Animals and people share the same houses.

A strong fence keeps out enemies and wild animals.

The chief's house is used for meetings.

Important dates

429-533	Vandal kingdom in North Africa
c.450-1066	Angles and Saxons rule parts of Britain.
456-711	Visigoth kingdom in Spain
481-511	Clovis rules over the Franks.
493-555	Ostrogoth kingdom in Italy
c.500-843	Frankish kingdom in France and Germany

EUROPE

500	600	700	800	900

Return to Christianity

A pagan god

Most barbarians were pagans who did not believe in Christ. Wherever they settled, churches were abandoned. By around 500, Christianity had almost disappeared in many parts of Europe.

Spreading the message

The leaders of the Church in Rome and Constantinople decided to send out monks to teach the Christian religion.

Monks were also sent from Ireland, which had not been invaded by barbarians. Slowly, the barbarians became Christians, and churches and monasteries were built all over Europe.

Irish monks set up carved crosses near their monasteries.

Irish missionaries

Monks and manuscripts

Most barbarians could not read or write, but the monks made sure that learning did not die out. They kept holy books in their monasteries and made beautiful copies of them. These handwritten books, called manuscripts, were often beautifully illustrated.

Monks working on manuscripts

An illustration from a manuscript called the Book of Kells

Augustine and the Angles

A monk called Augustine was sent from Rome to preach to the Angles of southeast Britain. Thousands of Angles became Christians and their leader, King Ethelbert, made Augustine the first Archbishop of Canterbury.

Augustine preaching to the Angles

King Ethelbert

The Rise of Islam

In the year 610, a man called Mohammed started to teach a new religion in Arabia. The religion became known as Islam, and its followers were called Muslims.

Arabia in Mohammed's time

Mohammed's message

Mohammed said that people should obey Allah, the one true god. He taught Muslims to pray five times a day, to give money to the poor, and to go without food and drink during daylight hours in the month called Ramadan.

Muslims going on a pilgrimage

Mohammed also said that all Muslims should try to go on a pilgrimage (religious journey) to Mecca, the holy city of Islam.

Mosques

Muslims pray in beautiful buildings called mosques. They are called to prayer by a man called a muezzin who stands in a tower called a minaret. Pictures of animals and people are not allowed in mosques. Instead, mosques are decorated with patterned tiles.

This picture shows Muslims praying in the courtyard of a mosque.

These towers are called minarets.

This is the mihrab. It shows the direction of Mecca.

The crescent is a symbol of Islam.

This is the minbar. A man called an imam preaches from here.

Muslims must wash in this fountain before they pray.

These people are praying. They kneel on prayer mats, facing Mecca.

This is the inner courtyard of the mosque.

The Koran

Muslims believe that Mohammed received many messages from Allah. Mohammed's followers wrote down these messages in a holy book, called the Koran.

Decorated pages from the Koran

The spread of Islam

Mohammed began preaching in Mecca, but rich merchants drove him out of the city and in 622 he escaped to Medina. In 624, an army from Mecca attacked the Muslims in Medina. Mohammed and his followers fought bravely and won the Battle of al Badr. After this victory, many people in Arabia became Muslims.

A scene from the Battle of al Badr

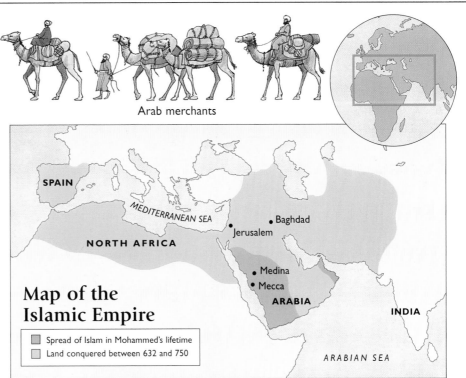

Arab merchants

Map of the Islamic Empire

☐ Spread of Islam in Mohammed's lifetime
☐ Land conquered between 632 and 750

SPAIN

MEDITERRANEAN SEA

NORTH AFRICA

Jerusalem • Baghdad

Medina
Mecca
ARABIA

INDIA

ARABIAN SEA

Conquering caliphs

After Mohammed's death in 632, the Muslims were ruled by a series of leaders, called caliphs. The caliphs fought many battles to spread their religion. By 750, they had built up a vast Islamic Empire, stretching from northern India in the east to Spain in the west.

A caliph's army in battle

Building mosques

Everywhere the caliphs conquered, they built mosques where people could pray. The Dome of the Rock in Jerusalem is part of a mosque that was built 50 years after the Arabs captured the city.

The Dome of the Rock in Jerusalem

The dome stands inside the Al-Aqsa mosque.

Traders and towns

The religion of Islam was spread by traders as well as soldiers. Arab merchants made journeys throughout the Empire and beyond, and, wherever the traders met, new Muslim towns grew up.

1100	1200	1300	1400	1500

The Arab World

In 750, an Arab family called the Abbasids became the new caliphs (rulers) of the Islamic Empire (see map on page 9). The people of the Empire were united by the religion of Islam, and many of them spoke Arabic.

Arabian wealth

The Abbasid caliphs collected taxes from people all over the Empire. They became fabulously rich and lived a life of luxury in a beautiful palace in Baghdad (in modern Iraq).

A caliph having a massage

Learning

The Arabs were keen to learn from other people's ideas. They collected books from all over the world and kept them in libraries. Arab scholars studied works from ancient Greece, Persia, India and China, and translated them into Arabic. They also wrote many books of their own and taught students in universities.

A scholar teaching students

City life

Arabian cities were busy and crowded, but they were also well organized. People prayed and studied in mosques, and washed in public baths. Markets, called souks, were held in the cities' streets.

This picture shows an Arabian city street.

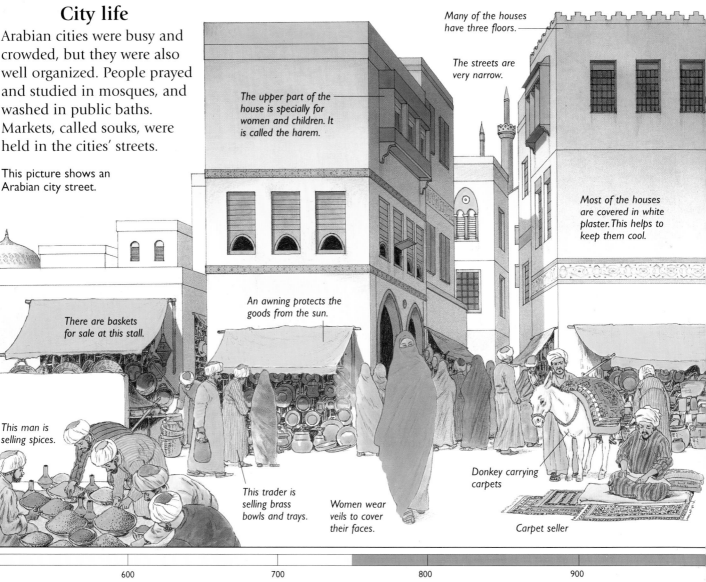

Many of the houses have three floors.

The streets are very narrow.

The upper part of the house is specially for women and children. It is called the harem.

Most of the houses are covered in white plaster. This helps to keep them cool.

There are baskets for sale at this stall.

An awning protects the goods from the sun.

This man is selling spices.

This trader is selling brass bowls and trays.

Women wear veils to cover their faces.

Donkey carrying carpets

Carpet seller

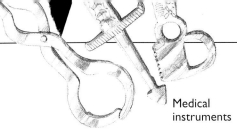

Medical instruments

Medicine and science

Arab doctors learned about diseases and performed difficult operations. Scientists discovered how to make steel and how to make drugs from chemicals.

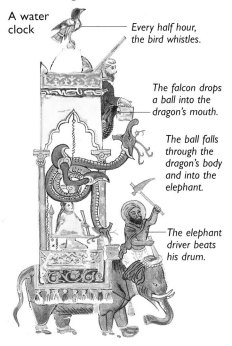

A water clock

Every half hour, the bird whistles.

The falcon drops a ball into the dragon's mouth.

The ball falls through the dragon's body and into the elephant.

The elephant driver beats his drum.

Inventors built amazing clocks, and engineers designed elaborate machines that were used to water fields.

This man is buying silk.

Sailing and exploration

Arab merchants sailed to China, Africa and India, and explorers set off on long journeys to distant lands. Sailors and explorers used special instruments to help them find their way.

A sailor using an instrument, called an alKemal.

An Arab sailing ship, called a dhow

Astronomy

Astronomers studied the sky at night and made maps of the stars. These maps helped sailors and explorers to find their way across seas and deserts.

Astronomers at work

Arabic numbers

From India, the Arabs learned a simple way of writing numbers, including zero. Until then, most people had used Roman numbers, which were very complicated and had no zero. The numbers that we use today are based on Arabic numbers.

٠ ١ ٢ ٣ ٤ ٥ ٦ ٧ ٨ ٩
0 1 2 3 4 5 6 7 8 9

Arabic numbers

The end of the Islamic Empire

Although the Abbasid caliphs called themselves the rulers of the Islamic world, their Empire was divided by the end of the 8th century. Separate kingdoms grew up in Spain, Egypt and India, and religious quarrels split the people of the Empire.

In 1055, an army of Turks captured Baghdad. The Turks controlled the caliphs until 1258, when a Mongol army invaded Baghdad, and killed the last caliph.

Important dates

c.570-632	Mohammed lives in Arabia. Most of Arabia is converted to Islam.
632-850	The first caliphs create a vast Islamic Empire.
750-1258	The Abbasid caliphs rule the Islamic Empire.
1055	The Turks take control of the caliphs.
1258	The Mongols conquer Baghdad. The Islamic Empire ends.

THE MIDDLE EAST

Vikings at Home

The Vikings came from Sweden, Norway and Denmark (see map on page 14). Their name probably means "pirate" and they were fierce raiders and fighters. In their own lands, the Vikings were farmers, fishermen and craftworkers.

A Viking farmer sowing seed

Farm life

Many of the Vikings were farmers. They grew crops and vegetables, and kept cows, pigs, chickens and goats. They also hunted wild animals.

Crafts

The Vikings were great metalworkers and carvers. They made elaborate weapons and necklaces, and beautiful carved objects.

Viking chesspiece

Viking homes

Thatched roof

Chest for storing clothes

The chief and his wife sleep in this bed.

Smoke hole

Wall hanging

This woman is weaving cloth at a loom.

Wooden frame

Carved door frame

This man is bringing wood for the fire.

In the winter, some animals are kept inside.

Toilet

Wall made from cane

This picture of a Viking longhouse has been cut away so you can see inside.

Most Vikings lived in large homes, called longhouses. Each longhouse belonged to a chief, and all the families who worked for the chief ate and slept in his house.

This boy looks after the pigs.

Death and burial

The Vikings buried people with food and treasure to take with them to the next life. Sometimes, a great warrior was buried on a ship. The ship was set on fire and people thought that it sailed to Valhalla, a kind of heaven where only warriors could go.

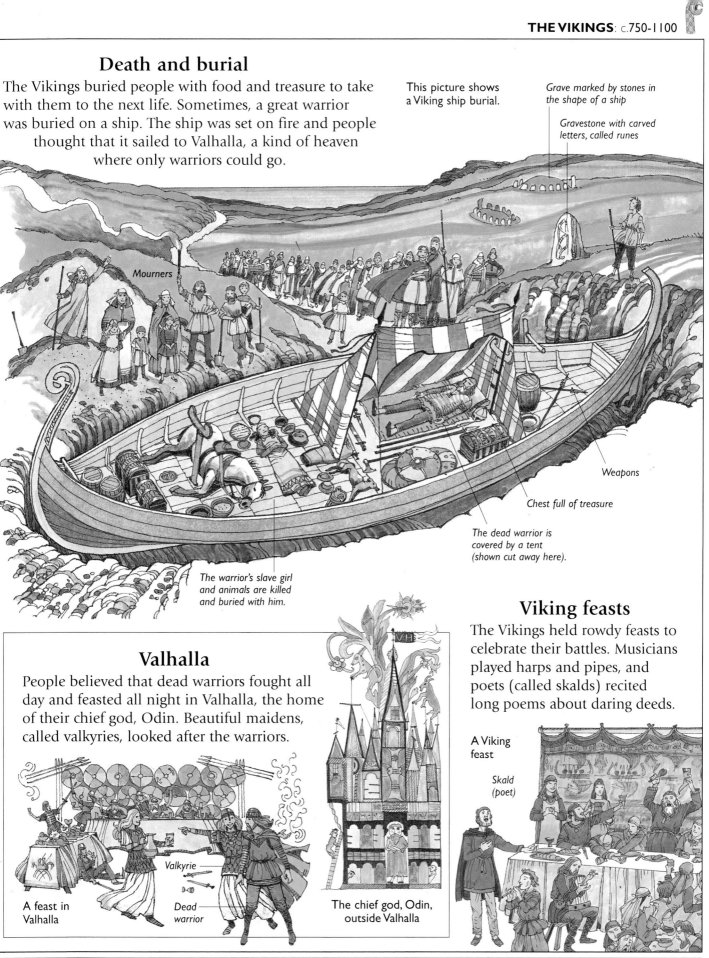

This picture shows a Viking ship burial.

Grave marked by stones in the shape of a ship

Gravestone with carved letters, called runes

Mourners

Weapons

Chest full of treasure

The dead warrior is covered by a tent (shown cut away here).

The warrior's slave girl and animals are killed and buried with him.

Valhalla

People believed that dead warriors fought all day and feasted all night in Valhalla, the home of their chief god, Odin. Beautiful maidens, called valkyries, looked after the warriors.

A feast in Valhalla

Valkyrie

Dead warrior

The chief god, Odin, outside Valhalla

Viking feasts

The Vikings held rowdy feasts to celebrate their battles. Musicians played harps and pipes, and poets (called skalds) recited long poems about daring deeds.

A Viking feast

Skald (poet)

Vikings Abroad

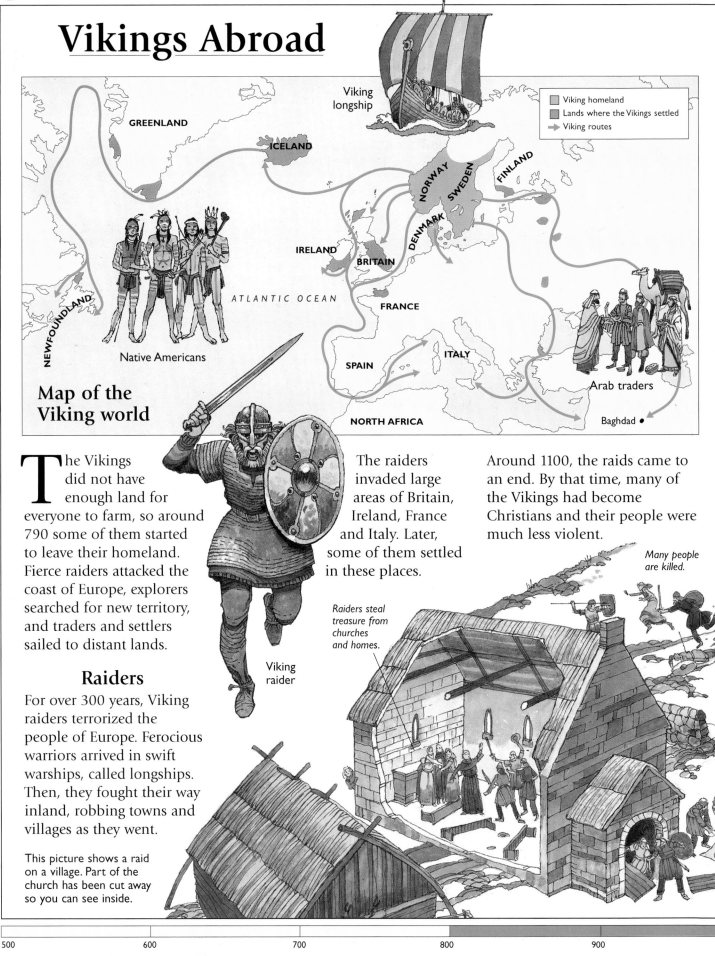

Viking longship

Viking homeland
Lands where the Vikings settled
Viking routes

GREENLAND

ICELAND

NORWAY SWEDEN FINLAND

DENMARK

IRELAND

BRITAIN

FRANCE

ATLANTIC OCEAN

Native Americans

NEWFOUNDLAND

SPAIN

ITALY

NORTH AFRICA

Arab traders

Baghdad

Map of the Viking world

Viking raider

The Vikings did not have enough land for everyone to farm, so around 790 some of them started to leave their homeland. Fierce raiders attacked the coast of Europe, explorers searched for new territory, and traders and settlers sailed to distant lands.

Raiders

For over 300 years, Viking raiders terrorized the people of Europe. Ferocious warriors arrived in swift warships, called longships. Then, they fought their way inland, robbing towns and villages as they went.

This picture shows a raid on a village. Part of the church has been cut away so you can see inside.

The raiders invaded large areas of Britain, Ireland, France and Italy. Later, some of them settled in these places.

Around 1100, the raids came to an end. By that time, many of the Vikings had become Christians and their people were much less violent.

Many people are killed.

Raiders steal treasure from churches and homes.

Explorers

Daring adventurers and traders sailed over seas and up rivers. When they could not sail any farther, the crew carried their boat, or dragged it on logs, to the next river.

Statue of Leif Ericson

Eric the Red explored Greenland. His son, Leif Ericson, went farther west and reached America. The land he found, called Vinland, was probably modern Newfoundland.

Explorers dragging their boat overland

Settlers

Boatloads of Viking settlers arrived in the newly discovered and conquered lands.

In northern France, the Vikings were called Normans (northmen) and in eastern Europe they were known as the Rus (redheaded people). The areas where they lived became known as Normandy and Russia.

A settlers' ship, called a knorr

Some Vikings settled in Iceland and Greenland. Others even went to live in Vinland (in America), but Native Americans attacked their homes and they soon fled back to Greenland.

Viking longships arrive swiftly and silently.

A lookout makes sure that it is safe to land.

The crew lower their sail and row ashore.

Some raiders seize animals and food.

This barn has been set on fire.

Some warriors take women as slaves.

Some people try to hide.

A few people manage to escape.

Native Americans attacking Vikings

Traders

Viking merchants traded in Europe and beyond. Some adventurous traders even reached the Arab city of Baghdad. The Vikings sold swords, fur and ivory (from walrus tusks). In return, they bought silk, precious stones, carvings, and beautiful objects made from gold and silver.

This eastern statue was found in Viking lands.

Important dates

c.790	The Viking raids begin.
c.830-900	Frequent raids on the British Isles and France
c.860	The Vikings settle in Russia.
c.900-911	The Vikings settle in Normandy.
c.983-986	The Vikings start a colony in Greenland.
c.1000	Leif Ericson reaches North America.
c.1100	The Viking raids end.

EUROPE

Anglo-Saxon England

Saxons arriving in Britain

Around the year 400, tribes of Angles, Saxons and Jutes began arriving in Britain from Denmark and northern Germany. These people were later known as Anglo-Saxons, and the land where they settled was called "Angle land", or England. By 600, England was divided into seven kingdoms, each ruled by a warrior king.

Map of the Anglo-Saxon kingdoms

SCOTLAND
IRELAND
ENGLAND
WALES
NORTH SEA
ENGLISH CHANNEL

— Border of the Danelaw in 878
▢ Northumbria
▢ Mercia
▢ East Anglia
▢ Essex
▢ Kent
▢ Sussex
▢ Wessex
The map shows the kingdoms in 800.

Thanes, churls and slaves

The Anglo-Saxon kings ruled over nobles (called thanes), farmers (called churls) and slaves. Thanes and churls were free, but they had to fight for their king. Slaves were owned by their masters.

A slave serving a thane at a feast

Village life

Most Anglo-Saxons lived in villages, although some of the villages grew into small towns. The men worked in the fields and went out hunting and fishing. The women cooked, made clothes and looked after the hens and pigs. Some villagers were potters, blacksmiths and carpenters.

This picture shows part of an Anglo-Saxon village.

Buried treasure

Some Anglo-Saxon kings were buried in ships, surrounded by their treasures. Helmets, weapons and jewels have all been found in the ship graves of Anglo-Saxon kings.

This helmet was found in a ship grave in East Anglia.

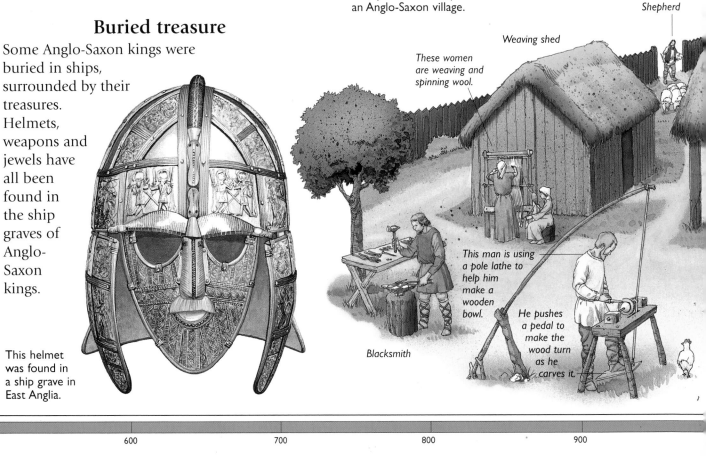

Shepherd

Weaving shed

These women are weaving and spinning wool.

This man is using a pole lathe to help him make a wooden bowl.

He pushes a pedal to make the wood turn as he carves it.

Blacksmith

EUROPE

500   600   700   800   900

Fighting the Danes

Around 800, tribes of Danes (Vikings from Denmark) began to invade England. By 874, they had conquered all the kingdoms except Wessex. King Alfred of Wessex drove the Danes out of his kingdom and won back Sussex, Kent and Mercia, which all became part of Wessex.

King Alfred fighting a Danish invader

Alfred the Great

King Alfred agreed that the Danes could settle in the eastern part of the country called the Danelaw, while he ruled the rest of England (see map). Alfred built strong, walled towns and set up a navy. He made fair laws and encouraged art, religion and learning. Later, he became known as Alfred the Great.

This jewel probably belonged to King Alfred.

Anglo-Saxons and Danes

In 924, Alfred's grandson, Athelstan, became king of all of England, but in 1013 the Danes invaded again. England was ruled by Danish kings for 30 years before the Anglo-Saxons regained control of their country.

Coin showing Cnut, King of England and Denmark

The end of the Anglo-Saxons

Edward the Confessor became King of England in 1042. He was a very religious man who rebuilt Westminster Abbey. When Edward died in 1066, Harold Earl of Wessex was crowned king, but he was soon defeated by the Normans, who conquered England (see page 20).

Edward the Confessor

Wooden fence

Thatched roof

Houses are built from planks of wood.

Well

Hen house

A thane lives in this hall. He holds feasts for all the villagers here.

Oven

Women cook soup in a cauldron.

Bread

Slaves roast a pig on a spit.

Musicians and jugglers arrive for the feast.

A fowler (bird catcher) brings birds for the feast.

Important dates

c.410-520	Angles, Saxons and Jutes settle in England.
c.600	England is divided into seven kingdoms.
867-874	The Danes invade England.
871-899	Alfred is King of Wessex.
924-939	Athelstan rules England.
1013-1042	Danish kings rule England.
1042-1066	Edward the Confessor is King of England.
1066	The Normans conquer England.

EUROPE

1100   1200   1300   1400   1500

Charlemagne's Empire

In 768, a young prince called Charles was crowned King of the Franks and inherited most of the land that is now France. (See page 6 for more about the Franks.) He was a brilliant soldier and a keen Christian, and he became known as Charlemagne, which means "Charles the Great".

Stained-glass portrait of Charlemagne

Map of Charlemagne's Empire

Aachen

WESTERN KINGDOM

EASTERN KINGDOM

MIDDLE KINGDOM

■ Lands inherited by Charlemagne
■ Lands conquered by Charlemagne
— Borders between kingdoms in 843

Building an empire

Charlemagne wanted to create a new Christian empire as large as the Roman Empire had been. For over 30 years, he fought for land, insisting that any non-Christians he conquered should join the Church. On Christmas Day 800, the Pope crowned him "Emperor of the Romans".

Pope Leo III crowning Emperor Charlemagne

Religion and learning

Charlemagne paid for churches and monasteries to be built all over his Empire. He encouraged scholars, artists and craftworkers to come and work in Aachen, where he had his palace.

Charlemagne's palace at Aachen

After Charlemagne

Charlemagne's Empire did not last long after his death. By 843, the Empire had split into three kingdoms, and each kingdom was ruled by a member of Charlemagne's family. The three rulers fought against each other and their kingdoms became very weak.

Important dates

768 Charlemagne becomes King of the Franks.

773-804 Charlemagne builds up his Empire.

800-814 Charlemagne is emperor.

843 Charlemagne's Empire is split into three kingdoms.

The Holy Roman Empire

By 900, all three parts of Charlemagne's old Empire were in danger. Vikings had invaded the Western and Middle kingdoms, and tribes of Magyars (from present-day Hungary) were attacking the Eastern kingdom.

Otto the Great

In 955, Otto I, King of the Eastern kingdom (now part of Germany), beat the Magyars at the Battle of Lechfeld. The Magyars were pagans who did not believe in Christ, and the Pope was so pleased by Otto's victory that he crowned him "Holy Roman Emperor".

Map of the Holy Roman Empire

Rome

SICILY

■ Frederick II's Empire
■ The Pope's lands

Emperor Otto's crown

Emperors and popes

After Otto, all the German kings had the title of "Holy Roman Emperor". They used their bishops to help them rule the Empire and had many quarrels with the popes over who had more power (see page 34).

The Wonder of the World

Emperor Frederick II inherited the kingdom of Sicily from his mother and ruled his Empire from there. Known as "the Wonder of the World", he kept wild animals, and welcomed astrologers and Muslim scholars to his court.

Emperor Frederick II

The Battle of Lechfeld

Magyar horseman

German horseman

Magyar foot soldier

German foot soldier

Important dates

955 The Battle of Lechfeld
962-973 Otto I is emperor.
1220-1250 Frederick II is emperor.
1250-1273 The Empire is weak.
1273-1291 Rudolf of Habsburg is emperor. He starts a new family of emperors.

EUROPE

1100　　1200　　1300　　1400　　1500

The Norman Conquests

The Normans were descendants of the Vikings who had settled in Normandy during the 900s. Like their Viking ancestors, the Normans were great sailors and warriors who were hungry for more land.

Map of the Norman conquests

Norman lands in 1130

ATLANTIC OCEAN

ENGLAND
Hastings
NORMANDY
FRANCE
ITALY
MEDITERRANEAN SEA
SICILY

Norman ships

Invading England

Duke William of Normandy believed he should be King of England because of a promise made to him by the previous English king, Edward the Confessor. In 1066, William sailed to England and fought King Harold of England at Hastings. The Normans were victorious and Harold was killed in battle.

King Harold of England

Italy and Sicily

The Normans also invaded southern Italy and the island of Sicily. In 1130, a Norman count became King of Sicily. For the next 60 years, the Normans ruled the island and the southern part of Italy.

Mosaic of Roger II, the first Norman King of Sicily

Norman horsemen fighting English foot soldiers at the Battle of Hastings

Ruling England

William was crowned the new King of England. He built castles all over the country and gave land to powerful nobles who promised to obey him.

Norman soldiers outside a castle

King William the Conqueror

Important dates

1060–1130	The Normans gradually conquer Sicily and southern Italy.
1066	The Normans conquer England and Duke William becomes king.
1130–1204	The Normans are kings of Sicily.

EUROPE

500   600   700   800   900

The Hundred Years' War

After the Normans had conquered England, the French and English kings fought many wars over who owned land in France. The longest of these was the Hundred Years' War. It began when Edward III of England claimed that he should be King of France.

Edward III

Edward III and the Black Prince

Edward and his son, the Black Prince, won a famous battle at Crécy, seized the town of Calais and captured the French king at Poitiers. By 1360, the English had won a lot of land in France (see map), but over the next 40 years, they lost most of it.

The Black Prince

Henry V

In 1415, King Henry V of England captured Harfleur and won the Battle of Agincourt. Henry planned to be the next King of France, but the French king's son refused to accept this, and fighting broke out again.

The French knights lead the attack.

This picture shows the start of the Battle of Agincourt.

Many French knights and horses are killed or wounded.

English archers shoot at the French knights.

Wooden stakes protect the English.

Jeanne d'Arc

In 1429, the French made a comeback. Led by a peasant girl called Jeanne d'Arc, they drove the English out of Orléans. The English burned Jeanne as a witch, but the French continued to win back land. In 1453, a French army captured Bordeaux, and the war ended.

Jeanne d'Arc

Important dates

1337 The Hundred Years' War begins.
1346 The English win the Battle of Crécy.
1415 The English win the Battle of Agincourt.
1429 Jeanne d'Arc drives the English out of Orléans.
1453 The Hundred Years' War ends.

EUROPE

THE NORMANS

FRANCE AND ENGLAND

1100   1200   1300   1400   1500

Kings, Nobles and Peasants

Life was very organized in medieval Europe. People were divided into four main groups and each group had different jobs to do. This way of life is now called the feudal system.

This diagram shows the four main groups in the feudal system.

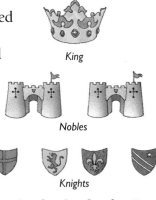

King

Nobles

Knights

Peasants

Knights

Nobles gave land to their knights as payment for their help in battle. Knights trained for war and fought for nobles and kings.

A knight training for war

Peasants

Peasants farmed the land of the knights, nobles and kings. In return, the landowners protected the peasants from enemy attacks. (To find out more about peasants, see pages 28 and 29.)

Part of a medieval calendar, showing peasants working in a noble's fields

Kings

At the top of the feudal system was the king. He owned all the land in a country, made the laws and led the country's army.

A king being crowned

Nobles

The king gave large areas of land to his nobles. In return for this land, the nobles promised to fight for the king and to provide him with knights for his army.

A noble promises to serve and obey his king. This promise is called "paying homage".

The people rebel

In spite of their promises to serve and obey, nobles sometimes rebelled against their king, and peasants led revolts against their lords.

King John and his barons

King John of England was a strong king with a fierce temper. He kept his nobles (called barons) under tight control, but in 1215 they rebelled. The barons made John sign an agreement called Magna Carta. This said that the king had to talk to a council of barons and bishops before he made any big decisions.

King John

The birth of Parliament

In 1275, English knights and townsmen joined the barons and bishops in a new council, known as Parliament. Over the next hundred years, several councils like this were created to control the kings of Europe.

A meeting of Parliament

The Peasants' Revolt

In 1381, hundreds of English peasants tried to win more freedom by rebelling against the landowners. Led by Wat Tyler, the peasants marched to London and rioted in the streets. King Richard II met the rebels and promised to help them, but later he punished them.

This picture shows the peasants rioting in London.

Peasants break into the Tower of London.

Houses are set on fire.

These men are stealing from a rich merchant's house.

These people are wrecking a lawyer's house.

This prisoner has been released from jail.

Some people are murdered.

Nobles and merchants try to escape.

Wat Tyler leads the peasants through the streets.

Important dates

1215 King John signs Magna Carta.

1275 The English Parliament starts to meet regularly.

1381 The Peasants' Revolt

EUROPE

Knights, Soldiers and War

Foot soldiers
defending a castle

During the Middle Ages, people had to be prepared for war at any time. Kings and nobles built castles to protect themselves from their enemies, knights and foot soldiers trained for war, and armies fought battles at home and abroad.

Defending a castle

A castle could be attacked by foreign invaders or by an enemy lord. Castles were designed to be extremely strong and easy to defend.

This picture shows an army attacking a castle.

Guards throw rocks over the battlements.

Castle guards pour boiling oil through here.

Archers fire arrows through these slits.

Soldiers use a siege tower to climb into the castle.

The drawbridge is pulled up to keep out enemies. (It has been cut away to let you see behind it.)

Some daring soldiers climb a siege ladder.

The portcullis is made of iron. It can be raised and lowered.

Battering ram

Some soldiers have built a bridge from planks and branches.

Pike   Catapult

Moat

Rock

This man is using a longbow.

500   600   700   800   900

Becoming a knight

Only boys from noble families could become knights. First, a boy worked as a page in a castle, learning how to ride and fight. Then, he became a squire and looked after a knight. When the squire had proved that he was a brave warrior, he was knighted by a king or a noble.

A noble knighting a squire

This is the pennant (flag) of the lord of the castle.

Stones from the catapult have damaged the castle walls.

This extra shelter was built just before the battle.

Soldiers use wicker shields to protect themselves.

Slingshot catapult

Rocks for the catapult

This man is loading a crossbow.

Knights in battle

Morning star

Metal helmet

Chain mail made from linked metal rings

Shield with coat of arms

Mounted knight

Knights fought on horseback, using swords, lances (long poles), axes, and vicious weapons called morning stars. Each knight wore a symbol, called a coat of arms, to show which family he belonged to.

Foot soldiers

Foot soldiers served their lord by guarding his castle and fighting for him. They fought with daggers, pikes (long spears), crossbows and longbows.

Medieval longbowmen

EUROPE

1100   1200   1300   1400   1500

25

Living in a Castle

Kings and nobles lived in castles with their families, their servants and their soldiers. In times of peace, the lord of the castle managed his lands, kept law and order, and held feasts and tournaments.

This cutaway picture shows the central keep (tower) of a castle.

These guards are looking out for enemies.

This bedroom belongs to the lord and his lady.

This is a private room for the lord's family. It is called the solar.

Watchtower

Keep

Inner bailey (courtyard)

Moat

Drawbridge

Gatehouse

Outer bailey (courtyard)

Plan of a castle

Chapel

This man is baking bread in an oven.

The castle guards eat here.

Well

Dungeon

Great hall

Stables

Garderobe (toilet)

Kitchen

Blacksmith

Knife grinder

Entrance

Food is kept cool in the storeroom.

Doves are kept in the dovecote.

500   600   700   800   900

Hunting

Kings and nobles often went hunting in the countryside around their castles. They rode on horseback with packs of hounds, and hunted deer, wild boar, bears and wolves.

King John hunting deer

Falconry

Falconry was a popular sport in the Middle Ages. Lords and ladies had their own falcons and hawks, which were trained by falconers to catch small animals and birds.

Falconers

Pastimes

Nobles and their families enjoyed dancing, singing and playing musical instruments. They played games, such as chess, and ladies worked on fine embroidery.

A game of chess

Feasting

Lavish feasts were held in the great hall of a noble's castle. Pages served rich food and wine, jesters told jokes, and minstrels played their instruments and sang. Many different courses were served, and a feast could last for hours.

Heralds will play their trumpets when the next course arrives.

This picture shows a feast in a castle.

The lord and lady sit under a canopy.

This is the high table. The most important guests sit here.

This man tastes the lord's food, to make sure it has not been poisoned.

The guests eat with their fingers.

Roast swan

Boar's head

This dessert is called a subtlety. It is made mainly from marzipan.

Salted fish on a pewter dish

Slices of stale bread are used for plates.

Minstrel

Jester

Tournaments

Tournaments, or mock battles, were often held in the castle grounds. The most popular sport at a tournament was jousting. In a joust, two knights charged at each other and each knight tried to knock his opponent to the ground.

This knight has dropped his lance and his shield.

The horses are called chargers.

Knights jousting at a tournament

EUROPE

Living in a Village

A peasant sowing seed

During the Middle Ages, most people lived in villages. A knight, known as the lord of the manor, owned all the land around a village and the peasants had to earn the right to farm some of his land. Some peasants were freemen, who paid money or food for their land, but others, called villeins, had to work part-time for their lord.

A nobleman lives in this castle.

The lord of the manor lives in the manor house.

This picture shows a medieval village.

The fields are divided into strips.

The lord of the manor is going hunting.

This is the pound where stray animals are kept. Their owners must pay to get them out.

The villagers keep their animals on a piece of land called a common.

Village green

This man is locked in the stocks as a punishment.

Inn

Stable

This man is fishing.

Well

Blacksmith

Carpenters

This man is cutting wheat with a sickle.

Farming

Most villages had three large fields. One was planted with wheat and one with barley. The third field was left fallow (unplanted), so it would be fit for planting the next year. Each field was divided into strips for different families to farm. A family would have several strips in each of the three fields.

These people are taking wool, eggs and cheese to sell in a nearby town.

Other jobs

All the villagers worked on the land, but some, like the miller and the blacksmith, did other jobs as well. People gave them food in return for their work.

EUROPE

500	600	700	800	900

The miller grinds the villagers' grain in this windmill.

Village homes

Peasants lived in simple cottages with bare floors and no glass in the windows. They had to share their home with their animals.

This cottage has been cut away so you can see inside.

Hole for smoke

Food for the winter is stored in the roof.

Thatched roof

Timber frame

Tools

Stable

Cooking pot

Stone fireplace

Clothes chest

People sleep on straw mattresses.

The walls are made from wattle-and-daub (twigs covered with mud and straw).

Church

Priest's house

Thatcher

Food

People ate bread, porridge, fruit, vegetables and stew, washed down with watery beer. Eggs, meat and fish were luxuries. Some families kept a cow and made cheese, but they sold most of their cheese at the local market.

A woman milking a cow

Fairs

At least once a year, a fair was held on the village green. Merchants came to buy and sell goods, people played games and held wrestling matches, and entertainers amused the crowds.

This woman is spinning wool.

Vegetable garden

Beehives

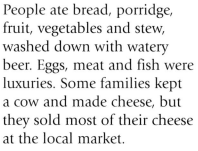

Acrobats

These men are wrestling.

Juggler

A village fair

This man has trained a bear to dance.

1100   1200   1300   1400   1500

Living in a Town

By the year 1100, small towns were starting to appear all over Europe. Many of these towns were built beside a castle. People living in a town paid rent to the lord of the castle, but they did not have to work for him and they could choose how to earn their living.

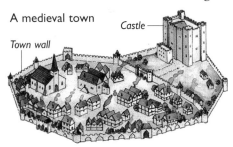

A medieval town

Town wall

Castle

Craftworkers

Many craftworkers set up workshops in the towns. They made useful things, such as clothes, pots and pans, which they sold to the townspeople and to farmers who visited the towns.

Dyers dyeing cloth

Merchants

Merchants sold wool, wood and iron to the craftworkers. They also sold luxury goods from foreign lands, such as silk, jewels, wine and spices.

A wine merchant's boat

This picture shows part of a medieval town.

Wine merchant's house

Church

Cloth merchant's shop

Farmers bring food and wool to the market.

Marketplace

People throw waste into the streets.

Brewer

Drain

The streets are very dirty.

Beggar

Inn

This is the potter's workshop. His family lives upstairs.

Other jobs

Bakers, butchers and brewers provided food and drink for the townspeople. Innkeepers ran taverns, and priests and doctors came to work in the towns.

Town visitors

Farmers and traders came to the towns to buy and sell goods. Everyone who visited a town had to pay money, called a toll, before they were allowed in.

500   600   700   800   900

Guilds

Craftworkers who made the same things began to group together in special clubs, called guilds. The guilds made sure that everyone made high-quality goods and that prices and wages were fair. Merchants also had guilds to make sure that they traded fairly.

Blacksmiths' guild badge

Joining a guild

Most members of guilds were men. Before a man could join a guild, he had to work for seven years as an apprentice to a master craftsman. Then he made his "masterpiece". If it was good enough, he joined the guild as a journeyman. Only a few journeymen became masters.

A master testing his apprentices

Holy days and mystery plays

On special holy days, the guilds put on plays for the people of the town. Sometimes, they performed a long series of plays based on Bible stories. These plays became known as mystery plays, because they were produced by craftworkers, and the medieval word for craft was "maisterie".

A scene from a play of Saint George and the dragon

A play of the Last Judgment

This wagon is called a pageant.

Angel

Guild sign

The mouth of Hell

Demon

Poor people live in cottages.

Houses often burn down.

This is the guildhall, where members of the guilds meet.

Baker's shop

Water-carrier

Shoemaker's workshop

1100   1200   1300   1400   1500

Traders and Towns

By the 1300s, people in Europe could buy luxuries such as silk, jewels, sugar and spices. The merchants of Europe traded with Arab and Turkish merchants, who sold goods from places as far away as India, Africa and China.

Jewels, silk and spices from the East

Merchant bankers

As trade increased, many people needed to borrow money to buy goods. A group of merchants from Lombardy in northern Italy created the first bank, and other Italians soon set up banks all over Europe.

Merchant bankers counting money

Trade fairs

Several times a year, merchants from all over Europe met at trade fairs to buy and sell goods. The towns where the fairs were held became very rich.

A bishop blessing a trade fair

Buying freedom

At first, townspeople paid rent to their local lord, but, as the towns grew richer, people wanted to be independent. In many towns, the people bought a document called a charter from their lord. The charter was stamped with the lord's seal to show that he had handed over his rights to the townspeople.

A seal on a town charter

Mighty merchants

Medieval merchants employed workers to make goods, such as cloth, and paid for splendid buildings to be built in their towns. The leading merchants of a town met in a group, called a council, and made decisions about the way their town was run.

The cloth merchants of Bruges paid for this market hall.

City-states

Some great cities in Italy and Germany had their own rulers who lived in palaces and made laws for their cities. These independent cities were known as city-states.

Venice was one of the richest city-states.

500   600   700   800   900

The Hanseatic League

Some of the busiest trading towns in Europe were grouped around the North Sea and the Baltic Sea. These towns formed a club, or "hansa", later known as the Hanseatic League. By 1350, there were over 70 towns in the league. All the towns helped each other and followed strict trading rules.

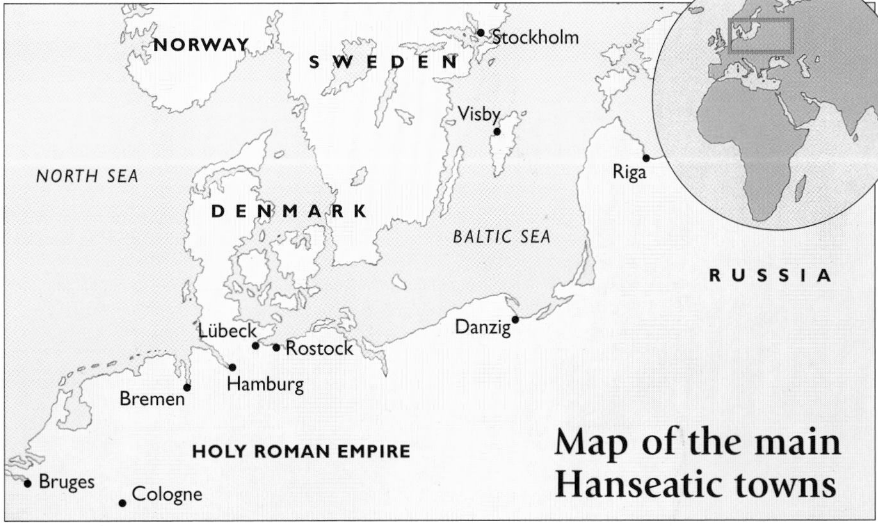

This picture shows a busy port in a Hanseatic town.

Map of the main Hanseatic towns

NORWAY

SWEDEN

Stockholm

Visby

NORTH SEA

DENMARK

Riga

BALTIC SEA

RUSSIA

Lübeck

Rostock

Danzig

Bremen

Hamburg

HOLY ROMAN EMPIRE

Bruges

Cologne

This ship is sailing to England.

This ship is carrying Chinese silk and jewels.

Rich merchant's house

Merchants store their goods in warehouses.

Wine

Some goods are sold at market stalls.

Crane

Bales of wool

Chests of spices

The merchant ships are called cogs.

Traders bring furs from Russia.

A clerk records the goods as they are loaded.

Wood and grain are loaded onto this ship.

Small boats called lighters take goods to the quay.

Wood from Norway

EUROPE

1100   1200   1300   1400   1500

The Power of the Popes

A medieval pope

The head of the Church in western Europe was the Pope, who lived in Rome. The popes wanted power over the rulers of Europe. They had bitter quarrels with the kings of France and the Holy Roman emperors. (See page 19 to find out more about the Holy Roman Empire.)

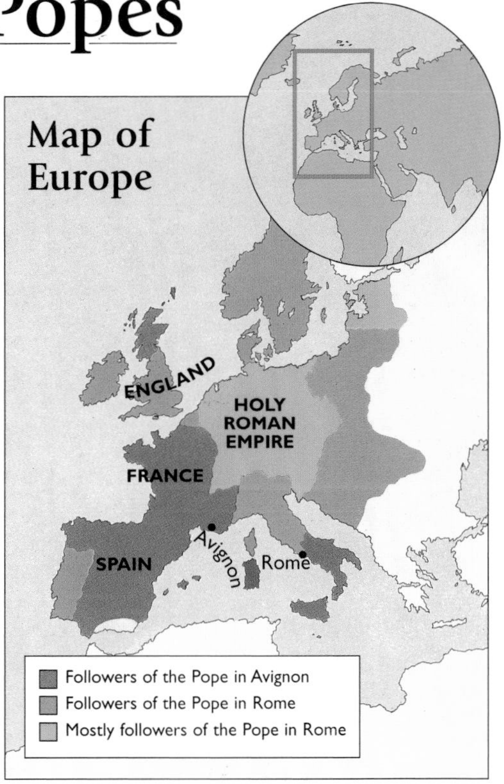

Pope and emperor

The popes and the Holy Roman emperors both wanted to control all the bishops in the Holy Roman Empire. This led to fierce arguments. In 1077, Pope Gregory VII made Emperor Henry IV wait barefoot in the snow for three days, before he would forgive him.

Pope and king

A French king, known as Philip the Fair, argued with Pope Boniface VIII over the king's right to collect taxes from lands owned by the Church. In 1303, Boniface announced that he had supreme power over all other rulers. This made Philip so angry that he took Boniface prisoner.

Pope Boniface

King Philip the Fair

Map of Europe

ENGLAND
HOLY ROMAN EMPIRE
FRANCE
SPAIN
Avignon
Rome

- Followers of the Pope in Avignon
- Followers of the Pope in Rome
- Mostly followers of the Pope in Rome

Popes in France

In 1309, a French pope moved to Avignon in southern France. The popes stayed in France for a hundred years, and, for part of this time, rival popes ruled in Rome. Some countries followed the Avignon Pope and others supported the Pope in Rome (see map). This split in the Church was called the Great Schism.

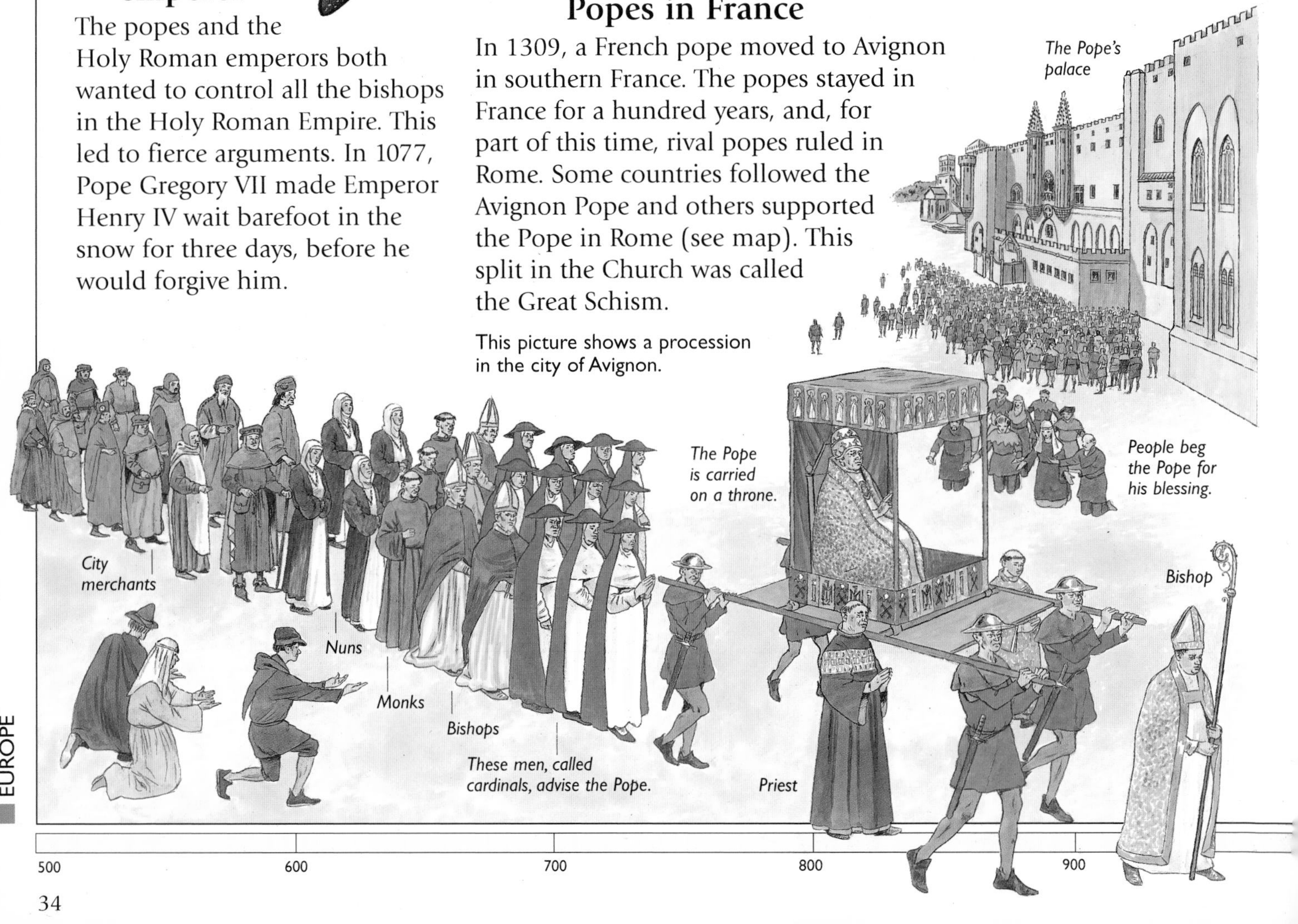

This picture shows a procession in the city of Avignon.

The Pope's palace

People beg the Pope for his blessing.

The Pope is carried on a throne.

City merchants

Nuns

Monks

Bishops

These men, called cardinals, advise the Pope.

Priest

Bishop

500   600   700   800   900

EUROPE

Enemies of the Church

In the Middle Ages, it was very dangerous to behave differently from the way the leaders of the Church expected. Anyone who questioned the Church's teachings was punished severely, people who acted strangely were accused of witchcraft, and Jews were cruelly persecuted.

Persecuting Jews

Jews had to wear special clothes so they could be recognized. They were attacked and killed all over Europe, and were driven out of England, France and Spain.

A medieval Jew

Trying witches

Suspected witches were given very unfair trials, such as trial by water. If they floated, they were guilty, and if they sank, they were innocent.

A suspected witch

Hounding heretics

People who questioned the teachings of the Church were called heretics. The popes sent out monks, called inquisitors, to find heretics and persuade them to change their minds. If they refused, they were tortured or killed.

Heretics being burned to death

Crusaders and Cathars

Crusader knights attacking a Cathar city

The Cathars were heretics who believed that the world was evil. Their ideas spread rapidly through southern France and this frightened Pope Innocent III. Innocent started a war, called the Albigensian Crusade, which did not end until all the Cathars were wiped out.

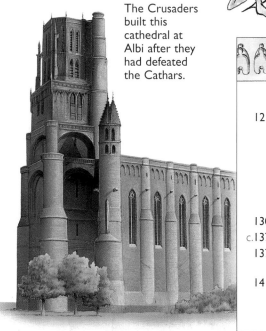

The Crusaders built this cathedral at Albi after they had defeated the Cathars.

Preacher power

Jan Hus was a Czech preacher who attacked the power of the Pope and said that people should read the Bible for themselves. He was arrested and burned to death as a heretic. After his death, his supporters, called Hussites, rebelled against the Pope and the Holy Roman Emperor. The fighting lasted for 17 years and the Hussites won many towns in eastern Europe.

Jan Hus being led to his death

Important dates

1210-1229	The Albigensian Crusade
c.1230	Popes begin to use inquisitors.
1290	Jews are driven out of England.
1306	Jews are driven out of France.
1309-1417	Popes in Avignon
c.1372-1415	The life of Jan Hus
1378-1417	Popes in Avignon and Rome (the Great Schism)
1419-1436	The Hussite wars
1492	Jews are driven out of Spain.

EUROPE

1100   1200   1300   1400   1500

Building a Cathedral

A bishop

Medieval bishops and archbishops gave orders that vast cathedrals should be built to show the glory of God. Most cathedrals took over a century to build. They were beautifully decorated with carvings, statues and stained-glass windows.

This picture shows a cathedral being built.

Stories in glass

Stained-glass windows in cathedrals and churches showed scenes from the Bible. Preachers used these pictures to teach people who could not read.

Window showing a scene from the story of Noah's Ark

Spire

Wooden scaffolding

A machine called a winch lifts blocks of stone.

The roof is covered with sheets of lead.

Sometimes, workers fall and are killed.

Workshop

Carpenters make benches for priests to sit on.

These men are mixing mortar (cement).

The master mason tells the workmen what to do.

The architect is showing the bishop a stained-glass window.

Stone cutters

Stone carver

Sculptors

EUROPE

500   700   800   900

36

Going on a Pilgrimage

A pilgrim

During the Middle Ages, many Christians went on religious journeys called pilgrimages. They became pilgrims to show their love for God, and because they hoped that God would forgive their sins and cure their diseases.

Pilgrim routes

Pilgrims journeyed to holy places, called shrines, where saints were buried or sacred objects were kept. Many people made the journey to Jerusalem or Rome, and pilgrims flocked to Compostela in Spain, to visit the shrine of Saint James, the patron saint of pilgrims.

Saint James

Canterbury pilgrims

In England, pilgrims went to Canterbury to pray at the grave of Saint Thomas Becket, an archbishop who was murdered by the knights of King Henry II.

The murder of Thomas Becket

Pilgrims' tales

Although the pilgrims' journeys were difficult and dangerous, they could also be fun. In the medieval poem "The Canterbury Tales", pilgrims tell each other stories as they travel along.

This picture shows pilgrims on their way to Canterbury.

Pilgrims stop at inns to eat and sleep.

Sometimes, robbers attack the pilgrims.

Monks

Nuns

This man is telling a story.

Sick child

Some people sing hymns.

This man is selling badges to pilgrims.

A priest preaches to the pilgrims.

Rich people ride on horseback.

This woman hopes that she will be cured.

This man is barefoot to show that he is sorry for his sins.

EUROPE

1100   1200   1300   1400   1500

Monks and Monasteries

A monk and a nun

Many Christians in the Middle Ages chose to serve God by becoming monks or nuns. They lived apart from the rest of the world in monasteries for men and convents for women. Monks and nuns prayed regularly, followed strict rules, and had special work to do each day.

This picture shows a monastery. Some of the walls have been cut away so you can see inside.

Visitors stay in the guesthouse.

All the monks eat together in the refectory.

Monks wash in the lavatorium.

Kitchen

Orchard

Vegetable garden

Monks care for sick people in the hospice.

Well

Monks copy manuscripts in the scriptorium.

This house belongs to the abbot, the head of the monastery.

Beehives

Meetings are held in the chapter house.

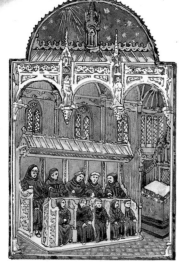

Monks praying in their chapel

Becoming a monk

Monks had to promise to give up everything they owned, to obey their abbot (chief monk), and not to get married. Before a man made these promises, he joined the monastery as a novice, learning its rules and getting used to its way of life.

Monks splitting wood

Saint Benedict's rules

Medieval monks followed rules that were written by Saint Benedict in the 6th century. He said that monks should pray, study, and work hard in the fields. They should eat plain food, wear simple clothes (called habits) and look after the sick and the poor.

Monks sleep in the dormitory.

Some monks work in the fields.

The monastery is surrounded by a wall.

This walkway is called a cloister.

Chapel

Altar

These poor people are coming to ask for food.

Fishpond

Healing the sick

The monks grew herbs in their monastery gardens and used them to treat people who were sick. They kept careful records of which herbs worked, and became experts at making medicines.

Monks preparing medicines

Making manuscripts

Unlike most people in the Middle Ages, many monks could read and write. They made handwritten books, called manuscripts, and decorated them with pictures and patterns.

A decorated letter in a manuscript

Wealth and power

Rich people gave money and land to the monks, and many monasteries became very wealthy. Some monks stopped living a simple life, and instead of praying and working hard, they spent their time running their lands, and enjoying a life of luxury.

A monk greedily helping himself to a drink

EUROPE

1100   1200   1300   1400   1500

Art in the Middle Ages

Most men and women in medieval Europe could not read, but they learned a lot by looking at pictures. People learned about Christianity from the paintings, carvings and stained-glass windows in their local church, and preachers used these images to illustrate their teachings.

Pictures in churches

Medieval churches were filled with images. Even the smallest churches had vivid paintings on their walls and simple carvings inside and out. Large churches and cathedrals were decorated with stunning stained-glass windows, delicate carvings and striking statues.

Painted statue of a German Christian princess

This window, which shows a coward running away from a rabbit, teaches people to be brave.

Curious carvings

Medieval carvers did not always show religious subjects. High up on church walls, they carved mischievous characters and monsters in stone. Some carvings on the outsides of churches had water spouts sticking out of their mouths. These carvings are known as gargoyles.

Carving of a monster

| 500 | 600 | 700 | 800 | 900 |

Art for the rich

Wealthy lords and ladies owned their own prayer books and Bibles, which were written by hand and beautifully illustrated. They also hung splendid tapestries on the walls of their castles. Many tapestries showed scenes of castle life.

A huntsman from a tapestry

Golden treasures

Goldsmiths made elaborate objects, such as crowns, goblets, and crosses, and decorated them with precious jewels.

Decorated top of a bishop's staff (stick)

Inspiring images

This 14th-century painting shows the Virgin Mary and Jesus surrounded by angels in heaven. It was probably displayed on an altar (table) in a private chapel.

Skilled artists painted beautiful religious pictures on wooden panels. These paintings, known as altarpieces, stood on an altar (table) in a church or chapel, and inspired people to worship.

The artists did not try to make their pictures realistic. Instead, they aimed to create an impression of heaven, by painting glowing scenes with glittering golden backgrounds.

1100   1200   1300   1400   1500

EUROPE

41

The Crusades

By the 1060s, Palestine, known as the Holy Land, was controlled by Muslim Turks. The Turks threatened Christian visitors to the Holy Land and attacked the Christian Byzantine Empire. When the Turks beat the Byzantines at the Battle of Manzikert (see page 54), Christians everywhere felt their religion was in danger.

A Christian artist's view of a Muslim warrior

Map of the Holy Land

▨ Crusader lands of Outremer

Constantinople

TURKEY

Edessa

THE HOLY LAND

Acre

Jerusalem

MEDITERRANEAN SEA

NORTH AFRICA

Saladin, a brave Muslim leader

The call to battle

After the Turks' victory, the Byzantine Emperor asked the Christians of western Europe for help. In 1095, Pope Urban II preached a sermon in France. He urged Christians from all over Europe to go on a crusade, or holy war, to drive the Muslims out of the Holy Land.

Pope Urban preaching in France

The First Crusade

Nobles from France, Germany and Italy gathered their armies together and set off for the Holy Land. It took them three years to reach Jerusalem, but in 1099 they captured the city and the surrounding lands. The Crusaders called these lands Outremer, which means "the kingdom across the sea".

The Muslims fight back

After the First Crusade, many Crusaders went home, leaving Outremer very weak. The Muslims seized the town of Edessa, and a Second Crusade failed to win it back. Under their brave leader, Saladin, the Muslims recaptured Jerusalem.

A battle during the First Crusade

Muslim soldiers

The Third Crusade

The Third Crusade was led by the rulers of England, France and Germany. They won many battles, and captured the city of Acre, but they did not win back Jerusalem.

Crusaders fighting Muslims during the Third Crusade

Crusaders ride heavy horses that are good at charging.

Muslim warriors ride lightweight horses, so they can attack swiftly.

Richard the Lion Heart, King of England, leads his army.

The Fourth Crusade

The Fourth Crusade only went as far as Constantinople, the capital of the Byzantine Empire. Although the Crusaders were supposed to be on the same side as the Byzantines, they attacked their city and stole many of its treasures. The Crusaders ruled Constantinople for nearly 60 years.

This picture shows Saint Mark's Cathedral in Venice. The four bronze horses were stolen from Constantinople.

Crusader knights

Groups of knights who were also monks were formed to fight the Muslims. The main groups were the Knights Templar, the Teutonic Knights and the Knights Hospitaller.

A Knight Templar

The end of the Crusades

Three more Crusades set out in the next hundred years. In 1229, the Muslims agreed that the Christians could take back Jerusalem, but this agreement did not last. The Muslims continued to win back land and in 1291 they conquered Acre, the last Crusader city.

Important dates

1071 The Battle of Manzikert
1096-1099 The First Crusade
1099 The Crusaders capture Jerusalem.
1147-1149 The Second Crusade
1187 The Muslims recapture Jerusalem.
1189-1192 The Third Crusade
1191 The Crusaders capture Acre.
1202-1204 The Fourth Crusade
1204 The Crusaders capture Constantinople.
1229 The Crusaders control Jerusalem.
1244 The Muslims recapture Jerusalem.
1291 The Muslims recapture Acre. The Crusades end.

THE MIDDLE EAST

1100　1200　1300　1400　1500

The Black Death

In 1347, a ship returned to Italy from Asia, bringing with it a terrible plague (disease). The plague was called the Black Death because of the deadly black swellings it caused. In six years, it swept across Europe, killing roughly one in every three people.

A sick sailor being carried ashore

Map of Europe

1353

BRITAIN

1348

RUSSIA

POLAND   1350

ATLANTIC
OCEAN

1349

1348

FRANCE

1347

SPAIN

The map shows when the Black Death reached different parts of Europe.

☐ Areas not affected by the Black Death

Fatal fleas

The Black Death was spread by bloodsucking fleas that lived on black rats, but no one realized this. People tried many ways to stop the plague from spreading, but nothing worked.

People burning the clothes of the dead

Punishment from God

Many people thought that God had sent the Black Death as a punishment for their sins. A group of men, called the Flagellant Brothers, tried to stop the disease by whipping their bodies to punish themselves. They went from town to town and actually helped to spread the plague.

This picture shows a town infected with the Black Death.

The owners of these houses have escaped to the country.

Thieves steal food from empty houses.

The dead are taken away in carts.

Infected houses are marked with a cross.

Some Brothers whip themselves.

A group of Flagellant Brothers walks through the town.

Rats run through the streets.

This doctor is trying to protect himself by wearing a leather mask.

Criminals and Outlaws

Life in medieval Europe could be dangerous and violent. Thieves lurked in towns, robbers lay in wait on lonely roads, and quarrels sometimes led to deadly fights.

Catching criminals

Groups of men took turns being watchmen in their towns and villages, but everyone had the right to catch a criminal. Anyone who saw a crime take place could chase after the wrongdoer, calling out to others to join in. This noisy chase was called a "hue and cry".

This picture shows a hue and cry in a village.

Wrongdoers are kept in this lock-up (prison).

The village watchmen join in the chase.

The pig's owner has started the hue and cry.

This man has stolen a pig.

Public punishments

Most punishments were carried out in public, to make people frightened of breaking the law. Wrongdoers could be locked in the stocks, or dragged through the streets and whipped, and people who committed serious crimes were put to death in front of large crowds.

A criminal being dragged through the streets

Harsh laws

There were many harsh laws in the Middle Ages, but some of the most hated were the forest laws. These laws allowed kings and nobles to hunt deer on their own lands, while any peasant who killed a deer was severely punished, and could even be put to death.

Outlaws

Sometimes, people ran away to escape punishment. These runaways became outlaws and lived in forests. They had no rights and it was not a crime to kill them. Many stories have been written about the famous English outlaw Robin Hood, but no one knows if he really existed.

Statue of Robin Hood

CRIME AND PUNISHMENT			PLAGUE		
1100	1200	1300		1400	1500

Kingdoms of the Celts

Celtic archer

By the year 500, barbarian tribes ruled most of Europe (see page 6), but some people, called the Celts, managed to stay independent. The Celts in Brittany remained separate from France until 1532, and the Welsh, Scots and Irish all fought to stay free of England.

Controlling Wales

The English kings wanted to control the princes who ruled Wales, so they gave land on the Welsh borders to powerful English nobles. These nobles, called marcher lords, kept the Welsh out of England, but also won Welsh lands for themselves.

Stained-glass portrait of a marcher lord

Welsh princes

Prince Llywelyn the Great united the Welsh princes and married the King of England's daughter. His son, Gruffydd, was taken prisoner by the English, but his grandson, Llywelyn ap Gruffydd, was accepted as the Prince of Wales by the English king.

Gruffydd falling to his death from the Tower of London

Celtic kingdoms

Marcher lords' lands in 1280

ATLANTIC OCEAN

SCOTLAND
• Bannockburn

IRELAND
Dublin •

ENGLAND

WALES

FRANCE

BRITTANY

Map of the Celtic kingdoms

The English triumph

Llywelyn ap Gruffydd gained control of most of Wales, but in 1276 King Edward I of England decided to fight the Welsh. Llywelyn was killed, Edward made his own son Prince of Wales, and the English built castles all over north Wales. After this, there were many Welsh rebellions, but none of them lasted for long.

Edward I naming his son Prince of Wales

This picture shows a Welsh army attacking an English castle.

English archers

The castle has high, strong walls.

Some English soldiers throw rocks.

Many of the Welsh are killed.

Welsh soldiers clamber up the cliff.

Wallace of Scotland

Scotland had its own king, but in 1296 the Scots could not decide who should be their next king, so Edward I of England took over as ruler. This made the Scots furious, and a Scottish knight called William Wallace led them into battle against Edward. At first, Wallace was victorious, but later he was captured and killed.

Statue of William Wallace

Most of the Scottish army are not trained soldiers.

Robert Bruce will lead his knights into battle.

Scottish knights

Scottish foot soldiers defend themselves with spears.

Bruce and Bannockburn

In 1306, Robert Bruce was secretly crowned King of Scotland. He defeated King Edward II of England at Bannockburn, and in 1328 Edward accepted that Scotland was an independent kingdom.

This picture shows the start of the Battle of Bannockburn.

The Scots have planted stakes in the ground.

The English knights charge at the Scots.

The ground is wet and marshy.

Some horses fall into pits dug by the Scots.

The English in Ireland

In 1160, an English noble, nicknamed Strongbow, went to help an Irish king fight against his rivals. Strongbow married the king's daughter and seized Dublin. This alarmed the English king who started a campaign to win Irish land for himself. By 1400, the English controlled eastern Ireland, but the Irish won back most of their land over the next hundred years.

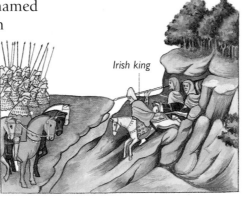

Irish king

Irish warriors attacking an English army

Important dates

1170	Strongbow seizes Dublin.
1258-1282	Llywelyn ap Gruffydd is Prince of Wales.
1301	Edward II becomes Prince of Wales.
1314	Battle of Bannockburn
1328	Edward II accepts Scotland's independence.
1532	Brittany becomes part of France.

EUROPE

| 1100 | 1200 | 1300 | 1400 | 1500 |

The Rise of Burgundy

One of the most powerful nobles in medieval Europe was the Duke of Burgundy, who ruled over an area, called a duchy, in eastern France. When the Duke of Burgundy died in 1361, he left no son to inherit his land, so King Jean II of France made his youngest son, Philippe, the new Duke.

Duke Philippe and his descendants built up a huge duchy in France and Flanders (an area now made up of Holland, Belgium and northern France). The dukes collected taxes from cloth merchants, bankers and farmers, and became incredibly rich.

Supporters of the arts

The dukes of Burgundy paid artists and writers to produce works of art. The famous painter Jan van Eyck worked for the Burgundy family.

The Arnolfini Marriage, by Jan van Eyck, was painted to celebrate the wedding of an Italian merchant who had settled in Flanders.

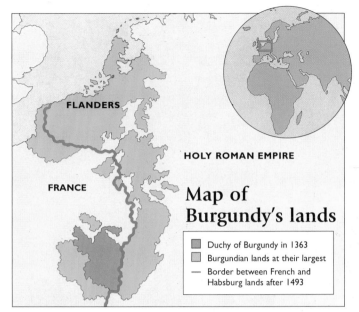

Map of Burgundy's lands

- ■ Duchy of Burgundy in 1363
- ■ Burgundian lands at their largest
- — Border between French and Habsburg lands after 1493

Quarrels in France

The dukes of Burgundy fought against the Duke of Orléans and his supporters, the Armagnacs. They also argued with the kings of France. In 1419, Duke Jean of Burgundy was murdered, probably on the orders of the French king's son. After this, Burgundy supported England in the Hundred Years' War against France.

Marie and Maximilian

In 1476, Duke Charles the Bold of Burgundy arranged for his only child, Marie, to marry Prince Maximilian Habsburg of Austria. The following year, Charles died in battle, and the French king seized some of his lands. For the next 20 years, Maximilian fought the French over Burgundy.

Maximilian Habsburg

Burgundy divides

Maximilian was crowned Holy Roman Emperor in 1493. In the same year, he and the French king agreed to divide Burgundy between them. The French took all the Burgundian lands in France, except for a small part of the original duchy. The rest of Burgundy joined the Holy Roman Empire.

The court of Burgundy

Magnificent feasts and dances were held in the castles of Burgundy. The knights and ladies of the Burgundian court wore extravagant clothes and had beautiful manners.

A dance in a Burgundian castle

The musicians play from the gallery (balcony).

This poet is waiting to present his work to the duchess.

Duke

Duchess

The duke's cup is held up high so no one can breathe on it.

This is the chancellor, who advises the duke.

Everyone at court wears fabulous clothes made from silk, satin, fur and velvet.

Important dates

1363-1404	Philippe the Good is Duke of Burgundy.
1410-1411	The Burgundians fight the Armagnacs.
1419	Jean the Fearless of Burgundy is murdered.
1477	Marie of Burgundy marries Maximilian Habsburg of Austria.
1477-1493	France and Austria fight over Burgundy.
1493	Maximilian Habsburg becomes Holy Roman Emperor. Burgundy is divided.

EUROPE

1100   1200   1400   1500

49

The Wars of the Roses

In 1455, a bitter struggle broke out between two branches of the English royal family. The opponents were the house (or family) of Lancaster and the house of York. Their struggle became known as the Wars of the Roses because both sides wore a rose emblem (or badge)

The white rose of York and the red rose of Lancaster

English royal family tree

✝King Edward III

- ✝Edward the Black Prince
  - ✝**King Richard II**
- ◑John of Gaunt, Duke of Lancaster
  - ◑John Beaufort
    - ◑John Beaufort
      - ◑Margaret Beaufort
  - ◑**King Henry IV**
    - ◑**King Henry V**
      - ◑**King Henry VI**
- ◉Edmund, Duke of York
  - ◉Richard of Cambridge
    - ◉Richard, Duke of York
      - ◉**King Edward IV**
      - ◉**King Richard III**

◉**King Edward IV**
◉Elizabeth of York
◉**King Edward V**
◉Richard of York

✝**King Henry VII** (also known as Henry Tudor)

- ✝ Plantagenets
- ◑ Lancasters
- ◉ Yorks
- ◉ Tudors

Lancaster weakens

King Henry VI came from the Lancaster family, but, unlike his father and grandfather, he was not a great warrior. He did nothing to stop the French from winning the Hundred Years' War and he could not control his nobles. He also suffered from periods of insanity.

Henry VI

The struggle begins

In 1454, Parliament gave Richard, Duke of York, the right to rule on King Henry's behalf. The next year, a group of nobles, led by Henry's wife, refused to let Richard rule. The Yorkists and Lancastrians gathered their supporters and began to fight.

A Yorkist king

Edward IV's symbol was a white rose inside a sun.

After a series of battles, Henry VI escaped to Scotland, and Richard of York's son, Edward, was crowned King of England. Edward IV ruled for 22 years, but he struggled against the Lancastrians for the first 10 years of his reign.

Warwick the Kingmaker

The Earl of Warwick helped his cousin, Edward IV, become king, but later he supported Henry VI when he tried to be king again. Warwick became known as "the Kingmaker".

The Earl of Warwick plotting against King Edward IV

Richard III

Edward IV died when his oldest son, Edward, was 12 years old. Before Edward V could be crowned, his uncle, Richard of Gloucester, declared himself king. Few people dared to oppose Richard, and he was crowned Richard III.

Richard III

Princes in the Tower

Richard insisted that Edward and his brother should stay in the Tower of London. The boys were never seen again and many people thought that Richard had given orders for them to be killed.

The young princes, painted by a 19th-century artist

The end of Richard III

The Lancastrians were determined to get rid of King Richard. Their choice for a new king was Henry Tudor, a member of the Lancaster family. In 1484, Henry invaded England from France. He fought against King Richard at the Battle of Bosworth Field, and Richard was defeated and killed.

This picture shows Henry Tudor leading his troops to fight King Richard III.

There are about 4,000 men in Henry's army.

The Lancastrian nobles support Henry.

Henry Tudor

Many men join Henry's army.

Some Yorkist nobles have abandoned Richard and joined Henry's army.

The first of the Tudors

Henry Tudor was crowned King Henry VII of England. He united the families of Lancaster and York by marrying Elizabeth of York, daughter of Edward IV. The Wars of the Roses came to an end, and England was ruled by the Tudors until 1601.

Important dates

1422-1461 Henry VI is king.

1455 The Wars of the Roses begin.

1461-1483 Edward IV is king.

1483 Edward V becomes king, but is never crowned.

1483-1485 Richard III is king.

1485 The Lancastrians win the Battle of Bosworth Field. The Wars of the Roses end.

1485-1509 Henry VII is king.

EUROPE

| 1100 | 1200 | 1300 | 1400 | 1500 |

Mongol Invaders

A Mongol yurt

The Mongols were nomads (wandering people) who roamed the plains of central Asia. They lived in tents, called yurts, and were always on the move, searching for grasslands where their animals could feed. In battle, the Mongols were cruel and bloodthirsty.

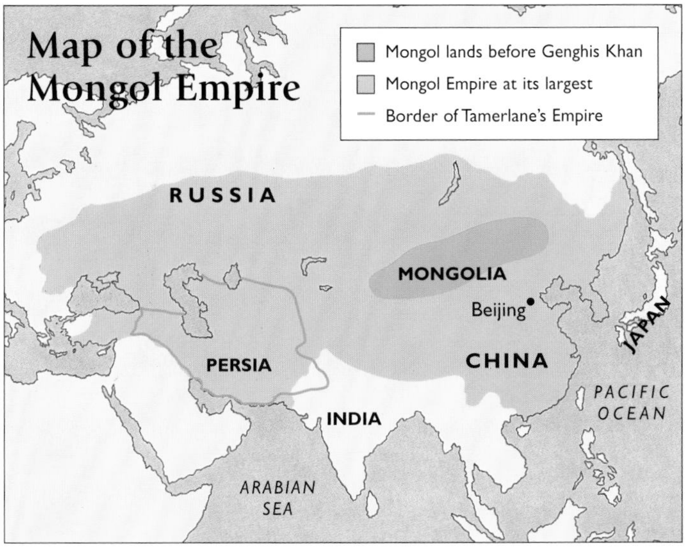

Genghis
Khan

Genghis Khan

Around 1180, a young Mongol warrior called Temujin began to lead daring raids on other Mongol tribes. He built up a powerful army and slowly brought all the tribes under his control. In 1206, the tribes named him Genghis Khan, which means "supreme ruler".

Building the Empire

Led by Genghis, the Mongols invaded northern China. Then, they swept eastward, killing thousands of people as they went. Genghis made laws for everyone in his Empire to obey, set up a messenger service, and encouraged trade.

After Genghis died, his sons and grandsons became khans (rulers). They won more land for their Empire in China, Europe and the Middle East.

Map of the Mongol Empire

- Mongol lands before Genghis Khan
- Mongol Empire at its largest
- Border of Tamerlane's Empire

RUSSIA

MONGOLIA

Beijing

JAPAN

PERSIA

CHINA

PACIFIC
OCEAN

INDIA

ARABIAN
SEA

This yurt belongs to one of the khan's wives.

Camels carry heavy loads.

These are the warriors' spare horses.

This is one of the khan's generals.

This picture shows the Mongol army on the move.

Some warriors wear breastplates and shoulder guards.

— Lance

This messenger is bringing news to the khan.

Guards protect the khan.

The khan wears a golden robe.

Warriors use bows and arrows, curved swords and lances.

Mongol horsemen use high saddles and short stirrups.

500   600   700   800   900

Kublai Khan

Kublai Khan was a grandson of Genghis Khan. He conquered all of China and made Beijing his capital city.

Kublai Khan

Kublai tried twice to invade Japan, but the Japanese resisted fiercely. He gave up trying to attack Japan when violent winds (called "kamikaze") wrecked his ships.

Japanese warriors attacking a Mongol warship

The khan's banner

This banner is made of horsetails. When they are in battle, the Mongols fly a banner of black horsetails.

The khan's yurt

Larger yurts are pulled on carts. Smaller yurts are packed up and carried by animals.

Catapult

The wheels of the cart need constant greasing with animal fat.

Teams of oxen pull the larger yurts.

These drummers beat their kettledrums when the army charges.

Tamerlane

After Kublai's rule, the Mongol Empire fell apart. Family quarrels made its rulers weak and many of the conquered people fought back. Then, in 1360, a Mongol leader called Tamerlane began to build a new empire. Tamerlane seized land in Persia, Russia and India, but the Empire did not last long after his death.

Tamerlane

Important dates

1162	Temujin is born in Mongolia.
1206	Temujin is given the name Genghis Khan.
1206-1227	Genghis Khan builds the Mongol Empire.
1259-1294	Kublai Khan rules.
1279	The Mongol Empire is at its largest.
1360-1405	Tamerlane builds a new Mongol Empire.

THE FAR EAST

1100   1200   1300   1400   1500

Triumphs of the Turks

The Turks were wandering people who came from central Asia. Around 950, a tribe of Turks called the Seljuks began to sweep westward. They invaded the Islamic Empire which had become so weak that its ruler welcomed the Seljuks into his capital, Baghdad.

Map of Seljuk lands

TURKEY
Manzikert
SYRIA
Baghdad
Jerusalem
PERSIA
PALESTINE
CENTRAL ASIA

Seljuk lands at their largest
Borders of the Islamic Empire
Borders of the Byzantine Empire

Seljuk warriors

Seljuks lived in tents called yurts.

Metal breastplate

Embroidered cloth

Winning land

In the 1050s, the Seljuks began invading the Byzantine Empire. They defeated the Byzantines at Manzikert and won Turkey. Later, they also captured Syria and Palestine (the Holy Land). Many Seljuks settled in their newly gained lands. They followed the Muslim religion and built elaborate mosques.

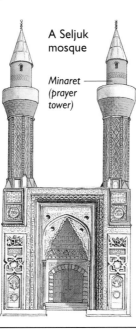

A Seljuk mosque

Minaret (prayer tower)

A Seljuk holy dancer, called a whirling dervish

The Crusaders fight back

Some Seljuks attacked Christian visitors to the Holy Land, and many Christians felt that they should fight for the land where their religion began. The Pope called for a crusade (holy war) against the Seljuks, and by 1100 the Crusaders had conquered most of Palestine (see page 42).

Seljuks attacking Christians

The end of the Seljuks

By 1200, the Seljuks had split into small groups ruled by rival princes, and many Seljuk people rebelled against their leaders. When tribes of Mongols attacked them, the Seljuks were too weak to fight back. By 1300, the Mongols had conquered most of the Seljuk lands except Turkey.

Mongol soldiers

500   600   700   800   900

The rise of the Ottoman Empire

In 1301, a Turkish prince called Osman declared himself Sultan (king) of all the Turks. He built up an army and began to win land. The land won by Osman and his descendants was called the Ottoman Empire.

Osman I

A public bath built for a sultan

Running the Empire

The Ottoman sultans were strong rulers as well as skilled soldiers. They made strict laws for their people, and built beautiful mosques, schools and baths in their cities.

Map of the Ottoman Empire

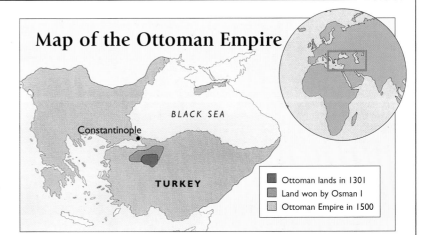

BLACK SEA

Constantinople

TURKEY

- ■ Ottoman lands in 1301
- ■ Land won by Osman I
- □ Ottoman Empire in 1500

The fall of Constantinople

The Ottomans gradually won land from the Byzantine people, and in 1453 they captured Constantinople, the capital city of the Byzantine Empire (see page 5). Sultan Mehmet II rebuilt Constantinople, which he renamed Istanbul, and made it the capital of the Ottoman Empire.

This picture shows the Ottomans marching through Constantinople after their victory.

Some buildings are on fire.

Prisoners of war

Many buildings have been damaged in the battle.

Mounted soldiers

Sultan Mehmet

Guards

The Byzantine people are scared.

Janissaries (foot soldiers)

Musicians announce the arrival of the sultan.

Important dates

1055 The Seljuks enter Baghdad.

1071 The Seljuks defeat the Byzantines at Manzikert.

1099 The Crusaders capture parts of Palestine.

c.1200-1300 The Mongols invade the Seljuk lands.

1301-1326 Osman I is sultan.

1451-1481 Mehmet II is sultan.

1453 The Ottomans capture Constantinople.

THE MIDDLE EAST

1100   1200   1300   1400   1500

Kingdoms of Eastern Europe

During the 6th century, tribes of warriors from Asia began moving west into Europe. The warriors were pagans who did not believe in Christ, and the people of Europe were terrified of them.

The tribes created many warlike kingdoms in eastern Europe. Most of these kingdoms did not last long, but some of them later became powerful Christian countries.

Warriors from Asia

Magyars in Hungary

In the 800s, a tribe called the Magyars conquered the area now known as Hungary. The Magyars fought fiercely to win more land, but in 955 they were beaten by the Germans at the Battle of Lechfeld (see page 19).

The Holy Roman Empire

After the Germans' victory, the Pope set up the Holy Roman Empire and made the German king its emperor (see page 19). The Pope relied on the emperor to defend Christian Europe against invading pagan tribes.

Map of eastern Europe

BALTIC SEA

Tannenberg

LITHUANIA

RUSSIA

HOLY ROMAN EMPIRE

Prague

Lechfeld

- Poland
- Hungary
- Bohemia
- Wallachia
- Lands of the Teutonic Knights

Crown of Charles IV of Bohemia

The kingdom of Hungary

In 975, the Magyar leader, Géza, became a Christian, and in 1001 the Pope accepted Géza's son, Stephen, as the first King of Hungary. Stephen was a keen Christian who was later made a saint. He created a peaceful kingdom with strong laws, and most of the Magyars became Christians.

This picture shows King Stephen leading a religious procession.

Churches have been built all over Hungary.

Bishops and priests accompany their king.

Count Dracula of Transylvania

Transylvania was part of the mountainous kingdom of Wallachia. In the 15th century, it was ruled by a count called Vlad Tepes, who was famous for his cruelty. Vlad put thousands of people to death by impaling (spearing) them on wooden stakes. He was given the nickname Dracula, which means "dragon's son".

Count Dracula

The kingdom of Bohemia

The kingdom of Bohemia (now the Czech Republic) was created by a tribe of Slavs in the 800s. It grew into a rich and powerful country. In 1355, the Pope made Charles IV of Bohemia the Holy Roman Emperor, and Charles moved the capital of the Empire to Prague.

The Teutonic Knights

The Christian kingdom of Poland was threatened by pagan Prussians in the north, so the Poles asked the Teutonic Knights for help. The Teutonic Knights were soldier-monks from Germany who had fought in the Crusades.

The Knights conquered the Prussians and seized their lands. Then, they tried to win more land in Poland, Russia and Lithuania. Eventually, they were beaten by the Poles at the Battle of Tannenberg.

This picture shows Teutonic Knights attacking a Prussian village.

Knights have set fire to the villlage.

Any Prussians who do not accept Christianity are killed.

Knights use rafts to cross the lake.

Some Prussians will be taken prisoner.

These Prussians are escaping into the forest.

Important dates

955	The Germans beat the Magyars at Lechfeld. The Pope creates the Holy Roman Empire.
1001	The Pope recognizes the Christian kingdom of Hungary.
1224-1239	The Teutonic Knights conquer the Prussians.
1355-1378	Charles IV of Bohemia is Holy Roman Emperor.
1410	The Poles defeat the Teutonic Knights at Tannenberg.

1100   1200   1300   1400   1500

The Rise of the Russians

Viking ship

Around the year 700, Vikings from Sweden began to travel down rivers into the area that is now western Russia. At first, the Vikings attacked the Slavs who were living there, but later they settled down and started to build towns.

Rurik the Rus

Around 862, a Viking leader called Rurik captured the Slavic city of Novgorod and the lands around it. Rurik's followers were called the Rus, from which we get the name "Russian". The Russians won lots of land and, in 882, Kiev became their new capital city.

The city of Novgorod

Map of the Russian lands

- Russian lands around 1000
- Borders of the Khanate of the Golden Horde
- Borders of Russia in 1505

SWEDEN
Neva
Lake Peipus
Novgorod
Moscow
Kulikova
Kiev
Constantinople

Vladimir the Saint

Prince Vladimir

Vladimir became Prince of Kiev in 978. He believed that he could turn people into Christians by forcing them to be baptized (washed in water as a sign of a new beginning). After his death, Vladimir was made a saint because so many of his people had become Christians.

This picture shows Russian people being baptized.

Yaroslav the Wise

Vladimir's son, Yaroslav, made Kiev into a rich and powerful city. He encouraged art and learning, created a strong government, and sent traders to Constantinople. Later, he became known as "Yaroslav the Wise".

Saint Sofia's cathedral in Kiev, built in Yaroslav's reign

Soldiers force people into the water.

500   600   700   800   900

The Tartars arrive

The Russian rulers who came after Yaroslav were weak, and in 1240 Kiev was captured by tribes of Mongols, known in Russia as Tartars. The Tartars created a vast kingdom called the Khanate of the Golden Horde, and forced the Russian rulers to pay them large sums of money, called tribute.

A Tartar warrior

Nevsky's victories

While the Tartars were invading the south, the Russians in the north defeated a Swedish army on the banks of the Neva, and drove back German invaders at Lake Peipus. Their leader, Alexander, became a hero. He was called "Nevsky" because of his victory at the Neva.

Nevsky leading his troops into battle

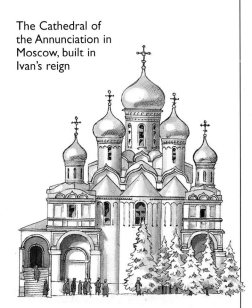

The growth of Moscow

Nevsky's son, Daniel, was crowned Prince of Moscow in 1280. Over the next 200 years, the princes of Moscow built up a powerful kingdom called Muscovy. Moscow became the most important city in Russia and, in 1328, the head of the Russian Church settled there.

Muscovite artists painted beautiful religious pictures, called icons.

The Tartars weaken

By the 1350s, the Tartars were fighting amongst themselves. Their kingdom split up, and in 1380 they were defeated by the Muscovites at Kulikova, in southern Russia.

Ivan the Great

The Tartars' power was finally broken by Prince Ivan III of Moscow. Ivan conquered the city of Novgorod and went on to win more land. In 1480, he declared himself Tsar (emperor) of all the Russians and refused to pay the Tartars any more tribute. He built many beautiful buildings in his capital city of Moscow.

Ivan the Great, first Tsar of Russia

The Cathedral of the Annunciation in Moscow, built in Ivan's reign

Important dates

c.700	The Vikings arrive in Russia.
c.862	Rurik creates a Rus kingdom.
1240	The Battle of the Neva
c.1250-1480	The Tartars rule southern Russia.
1380	The Battle of Kulikova
1480-1505	Ivan the Great rules Russia.

EUROPE

The Struggle for Spain

In 711, an army of African Muslims, known as Moors, crossed from North Africa into southern Spain. Spain had been ruled for 200 years by Visigoths (see page 6), but the Visigoths had become weak and were easily defeated by the new invaders.

Moorish warrior

The Moors move north

By 718, the Moors had conquered all of Spain except the mountainous kingdoms of the north. They also marched into France, but Charles Martel led an army of Franks against them. In 732, the Franks beat the Moors at the Battle of Poitiers, then they slowly drove them back into southern Spain.

Franks fighting Moors

Moors

Franks

Map of Spain

FRANCE

Córdoba

Granada

NORTH AFRICA

— Border of al-Andalus in 1000
☐ Aragon
☐ Granada
☐ León and Castile
☐ Navarre
☐ Portugal
☐ Valencia

The map shows the main Spanish kingdoms in 1250.

Learning and leisure

The Moors of al-Andalus were famous for their civilized way of life. They studied science, mathematics and astronomy, composed music, and wrote poetry. They also enjoyed playing games, such as chess.

Moors playing chess

The kingdom of al-Andalus

The Moors created a Muslim kingdom in southern Spain, called al-Andalus. The Moors were great traders and builders and their capital, Córdoba, became one of the richest cities in Europe.

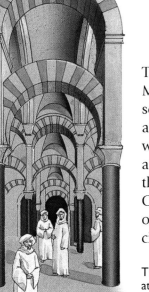
The Great Mosque at Córdoba

The rise of the Christian kingdoms

Around 1000, al-Andalus became weaker and began to split into separate kingdoms. At the same time, the unconquered Christian kingdoms in the north were growing stronger. In 1037, León and Castile were united, and Aragon and Navarre gradually became more powerful. In 1139, the new kingdom of Portugal was created.

A king of León

The Christians fight back

For over 450 years, the rulers of the Christian kingdoms fought to drive the Moors out of Spain. The Christians gradually moved south, conquering cities as they went. This long struggle to win back land is known as the "Reconquista".

El Cid

The most famous soldier of the Reconquista was Rodrigo Diaz, known as El Cid, which means "the Lord". He led daring raids into Muslim lands and seized the kingdom of Valencia, which he ruled himself.

El Cid

The kingdom of Granada

By 1250, the Christians had won back all of Spain except the Muslim kingdom of Granada. One reason Granada survived so long was because its sultans (rulers) paid large sums of money, called tribute, to the kings of León and Castile. It was finally conquered in 1492.

A sultan of Granada

This picture shows a Christian army marching into battle.

Battle tent called a pavillion

Foot soldiers with crossbows and axes

Mounted knights

Noblemen ride beside the army.

The nobles and knights are very richly dressed.

Drummer

Standard-bearer

Heralds blow trumpets.

The Alhambra Palace in Granada

Important dates

711 The Moors invade Spain.

c.730 The Moors rule most of Spain.

732 Charles Martel defeats the Moors at Poitiers.

c.1000 The Moors' power in Spain starts to weaken.

1037-1492 The Christians win back Spain (the Reconquista).

EUROPE

1100   1200   1300   1400   1500

Conquerors of North Africa

The land along the north coast of Africa was one of the richest parts of the Roman Empire, but in 429 it was invaded by the Vandals (see page 6). The Vandals forced the people of North Africa to pay very high taxes, and let many Roman cities fall into ruins.

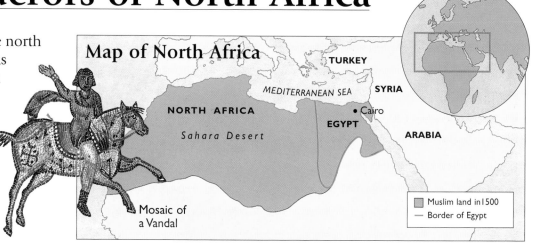

Map of North Africa

TURKEY

MEDITERRANEAN SEA

SYRIA

NORTH AFRICA

• Cairo

Sahara Desert

EGYPT

ARABIA

☐ Muslim land in 1500
— Border of Egypt

Mosaic of a Vandal

A Roman villa in North Africa

Byzantine rulers

In 533, the Byzantine Emperor Justinian drove the Vandals out of Africa. For the next 150 years, Byzantine rulers in North Africa tried to bring back the Roman way of life.

Coin showing the Emperor Justinian

Arab invaders

The Arabs invaded North Africa in 697, and by 750 it had become part of the Muslim Arab Empire. At first, North Africa was controlled by the Arab caliph (ruler), but slowly local rulers set up their own Muslim kingdoms.

Arab invaders

Fatimids in Egypt

In 969, a group of Muslims from Syria, called the Fatimids, seized control of Egypt. They set up an independent kingdom and their capital city, Cairo, became very rich. The Fatimids ruled for 200 years until they were conquered by the Arab leader, Saladin (see page 42).

Cairo's city gates were built by the Fatimids.

Minaret (prayer tower)

Many merchants came to trade in Cairo.

Mamelukes in Egypt

Saladin's descendants stayed in power for 80 years, but in 1250 the Mamelukes took over. The Mamelukes were Muslim Turks who had once been slaves in Saladin's army. The most famous Mameluke leader was Sultan Baibars, who prevented tribes of Mongols from invading Africa.

A Mameluke warrior

Important dates

429-533	The Vandals rule North Africa.
533-697	The Byzantines rule North Africa.
697	The Arabs conquer North Africa.
750	North Africa is part of the Arab Empire.
969-1171	The Fatimids rule Egypt.
1250-1517	The Mamelukes rule Egypt.
1261	The Mamelukes defeat the Mongols.

AFRICA

NORTH AFRICA
EAST AFRICA

500   600   700   800   900

Cities of East Africa

Around the year 1000, busy ports began to grow up on the coast of East Africa (see map). Merchants from Arabia, India and China sailed to these ports bringing tools, cloth, glass and china. In return, the Africans traded gold and ivory, iron and slaves, and even wild animals.

East Africans gave this giraffe to the Chinese emperor as a gift.

Stone bird from Great Zimbabwe

City of gold

People from all over southeast Africa brought gold to the city of Great Zimbabwe. The gold was collected in the city, then sent on to ports along the coast. The rulers of Great Zimbabwe became rich and powerful. They lived inside a walled fortress in the middle of the city.

This picture shows the fortress at Great Zimbabwe.

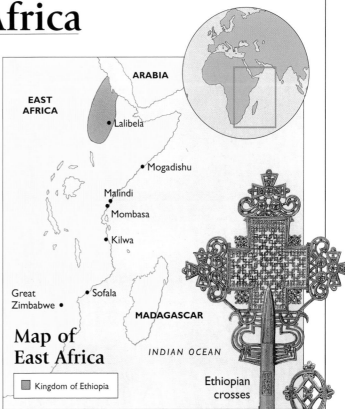

Map of East Africa

☐ Kingdom of Ethiopia

Ethiopian crosses

Religious ceremonies are held here.

The houses are made from clay and gravel, with grass roofs.

Strong outer wall made from granite blocks

The kingdom of Ethiopia

The Christian kingdom of Ethiopia was created around 1000. King Lalibela of Ethiopia believed that God had ordered him to carve churches out of rock. He built 11 churches which became very famous and the kingdom's main city was named after him.

One of King Lalibela's churches

Important dates

c.1000   The kingdom of Ethiopia is created.

c.1000-1200   Trading ports grow up on the east coast of Africa.

1200-1230   King Lalibela's churches are built in Ethiopia.

c.1350   Great Zimbabwe is at its largest.

AFRICA

| 1100 | 1200 | 1300 | 1400 | 1500 |

Kingdoms of West Africa

Arab merchants

By the year 800, Arab merchants from North Africa were crossing the Sahara Desert to trade with the people of West Africa. The West Africans grew rich by trading gold, slaves, and ivory from elephants' tusks, and many powerful kingdoms grew up (see map).

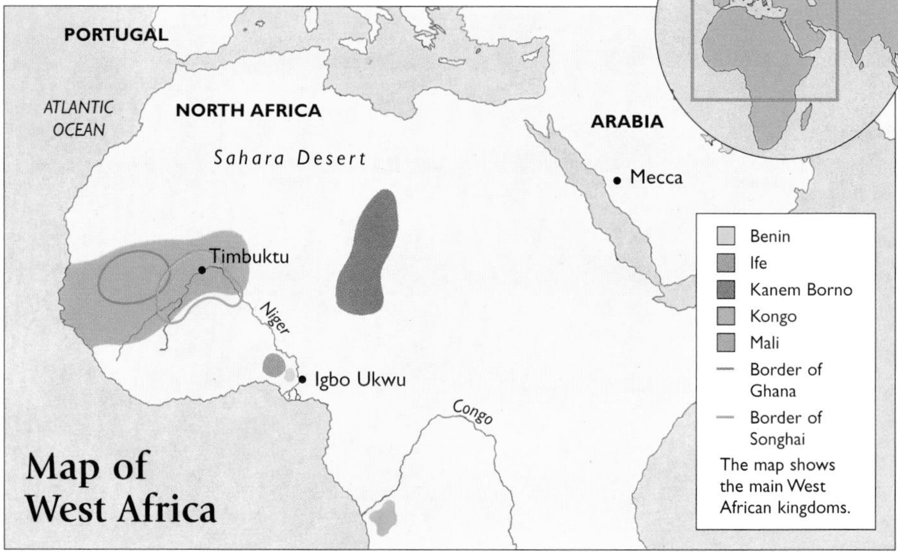

Kingdoms of gold

Between 300 and 1600, three great kingdoms rose and fell in the area south of the Sahara Desert. The kingdom of Ghana was followed by Mali and then by Songhai. Their people mined gold from rocks and their rulers became fabulously wealthy.

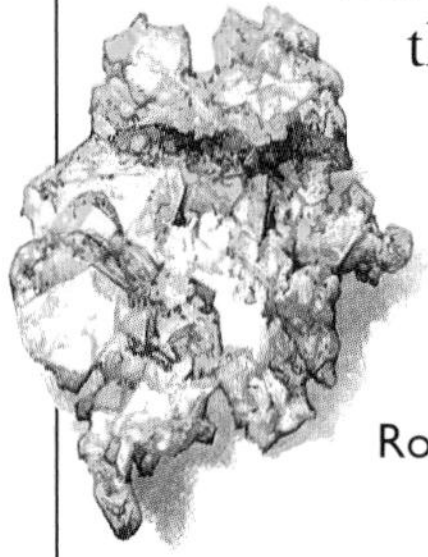

Rock with a crust of gold

Mansa Musa of Mali

The most famous West African ruler was King Mansa Musa of Mali. He was a Muslim and a strict, but fair, ruler. He went on a pilgrimage (religious journey) to Mecca in Arabia, giving away presents of gold as he went.

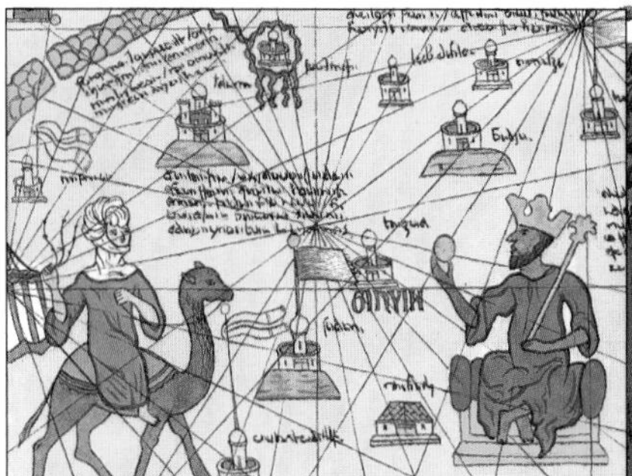

This map shows King Mansa Musa with an Arab merchant.

Map of West Africa

PORTUGAL

ATLANTIC OCEAN

NORTH AFRICA

Sahara Desert

ARABIA

• Mecca

• Timbuktu

Niger

• Igbo Ukwu

Congo

☐	Benin
☐	Ife
☐	Kanem Borno
☐	Kongo
☐	Mali
—	Border of Ghana
—	Border of Songhai

The map shows the main West African kingdoms.

The city of Timbuktu

Timbuktu was one of Mali's most important cities. It had a large royal palace, a famous university, and many beautiful mosques. Muslim scholars from all over West Africa came to study at Timbuktu.

This picture shows part of the city of Timbuktu.

The city is surrounded by a high wall.

Poor people live in huts with no windows.

Rich people live in large houses with windows.

Well

All the houses are made from mud.

Rulers of the forest

By 800, there were several kingdoms in the forests around the mouth of the Niger. Most of the rulers of these kingdoms were priests, as well as kings. A burial chamber found at Igbo Ukwu shows how priest-kings were buried.

Cutaway picture of a ruler's burial chamber

The kingdom of Ife

The forest kingdom of Ife (pronounced ee-feh) grew up around 1000. Its people were expert metalworkers who discovered a way of making figures from bronze. They made portraits of their past rulers and prayed to them.

Bronze head of a ruler from Ife

The kingdom of Benin

The richest forest kingdom was Benin. Its craftworkers made delicate ivory carvings and spectacular bronze statues, and its ruler (called an oba) lived in an enormous palace. Elaborate religious ceremonies were held at the palace.

A drummer at the oba's palace

The Portuguese arrive

In 1445, ships from Portugal reached the mouth of the Congo. Over the next 50 years, the Portuguese built trading towns along the West African coast. Some of the forest kingdoms, such as Benin, became very rich by trading with the Portuguese.

A Portuguese trading ship, called a caravel

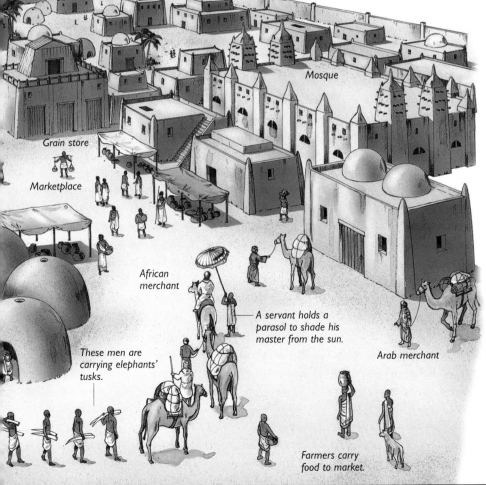

Grain store

Marketplace

Mosque

African merchant

A servant holds a parasol to shade his master from the sun.

These men are carrying elephants' tusks.

Arab merchant

Farmers carry food to market.

Important dates

c.300-1200 Kingdom of Ghana
c.800-1000 Kingdom of Igbo Ukwu
c.1000-1450 Kingdom of Ife
c.1000-1897 Kingdom of Benin
c.1200-1500 Kingdom of Mali
c.1312-1337 Mansa Musa rules Mali.
c.1350-1600 Kingdom of Songhai
c.1450 The Portuguese start trading in West Africa.

AFRICA

1100   1200   1300   1400   1500

65

Conquerors of Northern India

An Indian king

India split into small kingdoms around the year 550. These kingdoms were ruled by Hindu kings who prayed to many gods. The kingdoms of the south lasted for the next thousand years, but the kingdoms of the north were gradually conquered by Muslims.

Muslim invaders

Arab armies began invading northwest India in 711. The Arabs set up several peaceful Muslim kingdoms, but, around 1000, Mahmud of Ghazni led a series of savage raids on India from Afghanistan. Almost 200 years later, another Afghan, Muhammud of Ghur, conquered most of northern India. He killed hundreds of Indians and destroyed many Hindu temples.

Map of India

- ■ Sultanate of Delhi around 1300
- — Border of the Chola kingdom
- ▢ Kingdom of Vijayanagar around 1500

Sultans of Delhi

In 1206, a Turkish soldier called Aibak took control of northern India and made himself Sultan (king) of Delhi. The sultans ruled for the next 300 years. They were great builders, but cruel rulers.

Sultan Aibak built this tower to celebrate his victories.

Mongol raiders

In 1398, the Mongol leader Tamerlane led a savage attack on the city of Delhi. The Mongols massacred most of the people of Delhi and left the sultans very weak.

Indian troops fighting Afghan invaders

Hindu temple

The Afghans surround the Indians.

The Afghans ride swift horses.

The Indian war elephants move very slowly.

Kingdoms of Southern India

The Hindu kings of southern India lived in beautiful palaces surrounded by towering temples. Holy men, called brahmans, helped the kings to govern, and hundreds of servants worked in the palaces and temples.

This picture shows an Indian king and his court.

Hindu temple

Servants fan the king.

King

Brahmans (holy men) advise the king.

Musicians

Dancers perform a sacred dance.

The Chola kingdom

One of the most successful southern kingdoms was Chola. Its kings built up a great empire and sent merchants to Arabia and China. Chola craftworkers were famous for their graceful bronze statues.

Chola statue of a Hindu god

Vijayanagar fights back

Around 1300, the Muslim sultans of Delhi began to attack southern India. They won land rapidly until 1336 when two brothers created the new Hindu kingdom of Vijayanagar. The new kingdom's army soon defeated the Muslims, and Vijayanagar became the most powerful kingdom in the south.

Buddhist teachers

Although the kings of southern India were Hindus, they allowed Buddhist monks to set up universities and teach their religion. Buddhism spread from India all over Southeast Asia, and many Chinese Buddhists came to study in India.

Buddhist monks in Sri Lanka

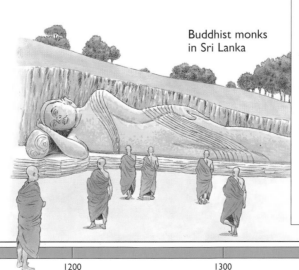

Important dates

711	Arabs start to invade northern India.
886-1267	The Chola kings control most of southern India.
1001-1026	Mahmud of Ghazni leads raids on northern India.
1193	Muhammud of Ghur conquers northern India.
1206-1526	The sultans of Delhi control most of northern India.
1336-1565	The kingdom of Vijayanagar is successful.
1398	The Mongols invade northern India.

SOUTH ASIA

1100   1200   1300   1400   1500

Kingdoms of Southeast Asia

Traders from India began arriving in Southeast Asia during the 2nd century. The local people learned about the Indian way of life, and set up small kingdoms like the ones in India. By the 800s, there were several powerful kingdoms on the mainland and islands of Southeast Asia.

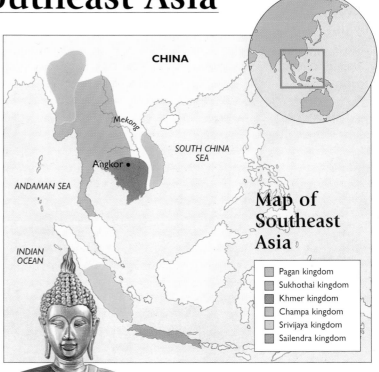

CHINA

Mekong

SOUTH CHINA SEA

Angkor •

ANDAMAN SEA

INDIAN OCEAN

Map of Southeast Asia

- Pagan kingdom
- Sukhothai kingdom
- Khmer kingdom
- Champa kingdom
- Srivijaya kingdom
- Sailendra kingdom

A king of the Sukhothai kingdom

Hindus

The Hindu religion spread from India throughout Southeast Asia, and the kings built magnificent temples where their people could worship Hindu gods. The people also prayed to their kings, who they thought of as gods.

People bringing gifts to a Hindu temple

Statue of the Buddha from the Sukhothai kingdom

Buddhists

Around the year 300, Buddhist monks from India brought their religion to Southeast Asia. Buddhism was popular, but it did not destroy the Hindu religion, and most of the kingdoms had temples for Hindus as well as for Buddhists.

Warring kingdoms

The kings of Southeast Asia were often at war with each other. Sometimes, warriors sailed over seas or along rivers to make surprise attacks on another kingdom.

Warriors from the Champa kingdom rowing up a river

THE FAR EAST

500   600   700   800   900

The Khmer kingdom

The greatest kingdom in Southeast Asia was ruled by the Khmers. Their capital city, Angkor, housed half a million people and was built close to a lake. The people of Angkor dug reservoirs to hold floodwater from the lake, and their farmers used the water to grow rice all through the year.

This picture shows a procession in the city of Angkor.

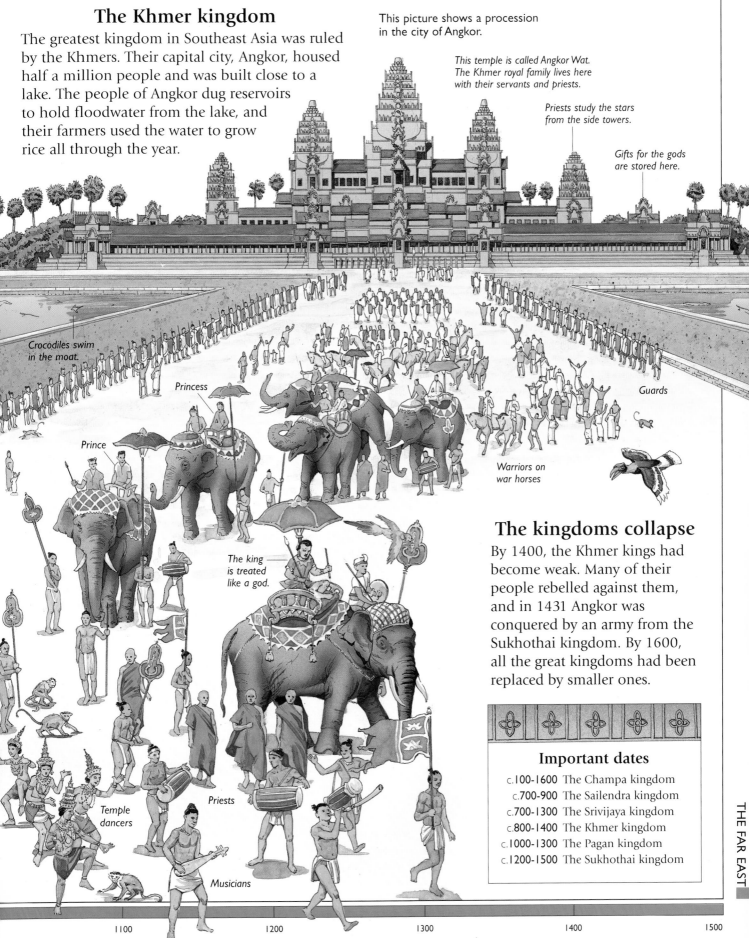

This temple is called Angkor Wat. The Khmer royal family lives here with their servants and priests.

Priests study the stars from the side towers.

Gifts for the gods are stored here.

Crocodiles swim in the moat.

Princess

Prince

Guards

Warriors on war horses

The king is treated like a god.

Temple dancers

Priests

Musicians

The kingdoms collapse

By 1400, the Khmer kings had become weak. Many of their people rebelled against them, and in 1431 Angkor was conquered by an army from the Sukhothai kingdom. By 1600, all the great kingdoms had been replaced by smaller ones.

Important dates

c.100-1600 The Champa kingdom
c.700-900 The Sailendra kingdom
c.700-1300 The Srivijaya kingdom
c.800-1400 The Khmer kingdom
c.1000-1300 The Pagan kingdom
c.1200-1500 The Sukhothai kingdom

THE FAR EAST

| 1100 | 1200 | 1300 | 1400 | 1500 |

Dynasties of China

In 581, a ruling family (or dynasty) called the Sui took control of China. The Sui emperors built a network of canals, which made it much easier for merchants to travel around the country.

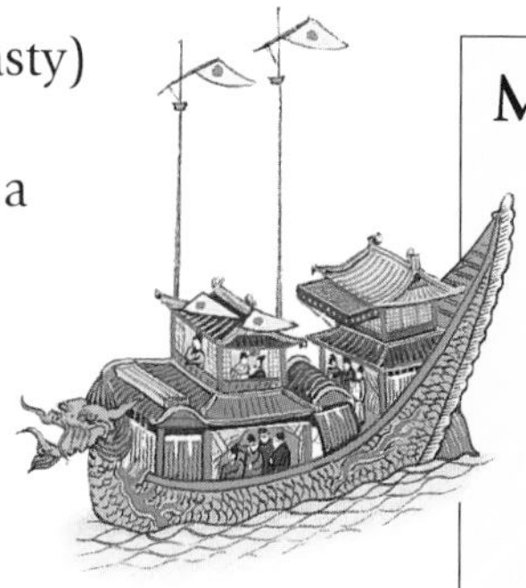

A Sui emperor's canal boat

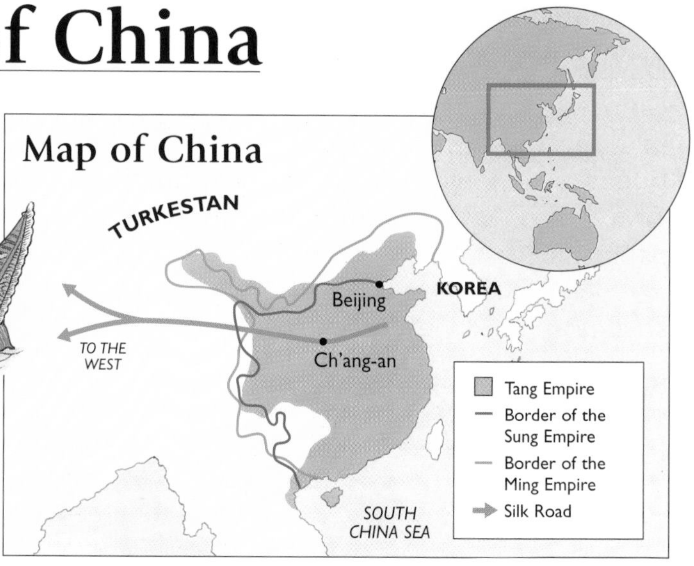

A Tang emperor

The Tang dynasty

In 618, a new dynasty, called the Tang, took over. The Tang emperors ruled China for 300 years and created an empire that stretched from Korea to Turkestan. The capital of the Tang Empire was the splendid city of Ch'ang-an. Nearly two million people lived inside its walls.

Map of China

TURKESTAN

TO THE WEST

Beijing

KOREA

Ch'ang-an

SOUTH CHINA SEA

▢ Tang Empire
— Border of the Sung Empire
— Border of the Ming Empire
→ Silk Road

The city is divided into walled areas called wards.

Pagoda (Buddhist tower)

Emperor's palace

This picture shows part of the city of Ch'ang-an.

Food stall

Beggar

Merchants sell silk, tea and spices.

Potter's workshop

Farmers bring food to market.

A poet reciting his poems

These gates are locked at night.

Foreign merchants visit the city.

Canal   Merchant's boat

Tang inventions

During the Tang period, the Chinese discovered how to make gunpowder and a kind of fine pottery now called china. They also began to print on paper, using wooden stamps.

At first, gunpowder was only used for fireworks.

The Sung dynasty

By 900, the Tang emperors had beome very weak, and in 960 the Sung family took control of China. Under the Sung emperors, the Chinese had little contact with the outside world, but they continued to produce beautiful china and paintings.

Sung artists often painted scenes from daily life.

The Ming dynasty

In 1368, a Buddhist monk called Chu Yuan-chang led a rebellion against the Mongols and started the Ming dynasty. The Ming emperors built up a strong army and encouraged trade, exploration and art. They ruled from Beijing, which became one of the world's greatest cities.

Ming china is famous for its delicate patterns.

Adventurous traders

Chinese trading ship, called a junk

Chinese merchants sailed as far away as Africa and also journeyed overland on a route known as the Silk Road. Traders on the Silk Road took silk, china and paper to the Middle East and Europe.

Mongol invaders

In 1211, tribes of Mongols began to invade China, and in 1279 the Mongol leader, Kublai Khan, became emperor (see page 53). Kublai Khan was visited by Marco Polo, a young merchant from Venice, who wrote about his travels in China.

Marco Polo at Kublai Khan's palace

Marco Polo brings gifts.

Kublai Khan

Guards

Chinese courtiers

Important dates

581-617 The Sui dynasty
618-906 The Tang dynasty
960-1279 The Sung dynasty
1275-1292 Marco Polo visits China.
1280-1368 The Mongols rule China.
1368-1644 The Ming dynasty

1100   1200   1300   1400   1500

Land of the Samurai

Chinese-style pagoda at Nara

By the year 500, a family of emperors called the Yamatos controlled most of Japan. They admired the way the Chinese emperors ruled China and they built their capital city, Nara, to look like the Chinese city of Ch'ang-an. (See pages 70 and 71 to find out more about China.)

Shinto and Buddhism

Entrance to a Shinto shrine

Shinto was the local religion of Japan. Its followers believed in spirits that lived in rocks, trees and streams. Around 600, Buddhist monks from China and Korea brought their religion to Japan. Buddhism spread fast, but Shinto did not die out.

Japanese statue of the Buddha

The emperor's court

In 784, the emperor moved his court to Heian (modern Kyoto), where he lived a life of luxury, cut off from ordinary people. Many clever women lived at the court and one of these courtiers, Lady Murasaki Shikibu, wrote the world's first novel, called "The Tale of Genji".

The emperor and his courtiers at Heian

Map of Japan

CHINA

SEA OF JAPAN

KOREA

Heian

Nara

JAPAN

PACIFIC OCEAN

Buddhist pagoda

Emperor's palace

Nursemaid

Emperor's children

Buddhist priests

Tea house

Lily pond

Emperor

A poet reads his poem aloud.

Emperor's advisers

Musicians

Servants bring food.

These court ladies accompany the empress.

Courtiers drink tea.

Empress

500   600   700   800   900

Nobles and shoguns

The emperors gradually gave away land to noble families. At first, the Fujiwara family were very powerful, but in 1192 the Minamatos gained control of Japan. The emperor made Minamato Yoritomo the first shogun, or military commander. For the next 700 years, shoguns were the real rulers of Japan.

Minamato Yoritomo, the first shogun

No plays

Actors performed dramas, called "No" plays, to entertain noble families. The actors were all men, and wore masks to show what sort of characters they played. A No play combined music, singing, dancing and poetry.

No masks

Jobs in Japan

Rice farmers working in flooded fields, called paddy fields

Most Japanese people were rice farmers who worked on their lord's land. Others worked as fishermen, miners, paper-makers, silk-makers, sword-makers and carpenters. Farmers and craftworkers took their goods to sell in the towns.

Sword-makers sharpening blades

Samurai armies

The shoguns relied on local lords to rule the country. Each lord had an army of warriors, called samurai. The samurai fought fiercely for their lord and were willing to die for him. They also drove away foreign invaders, such as the Mongols (see page 53).

This picture shows samurai riding into battle.

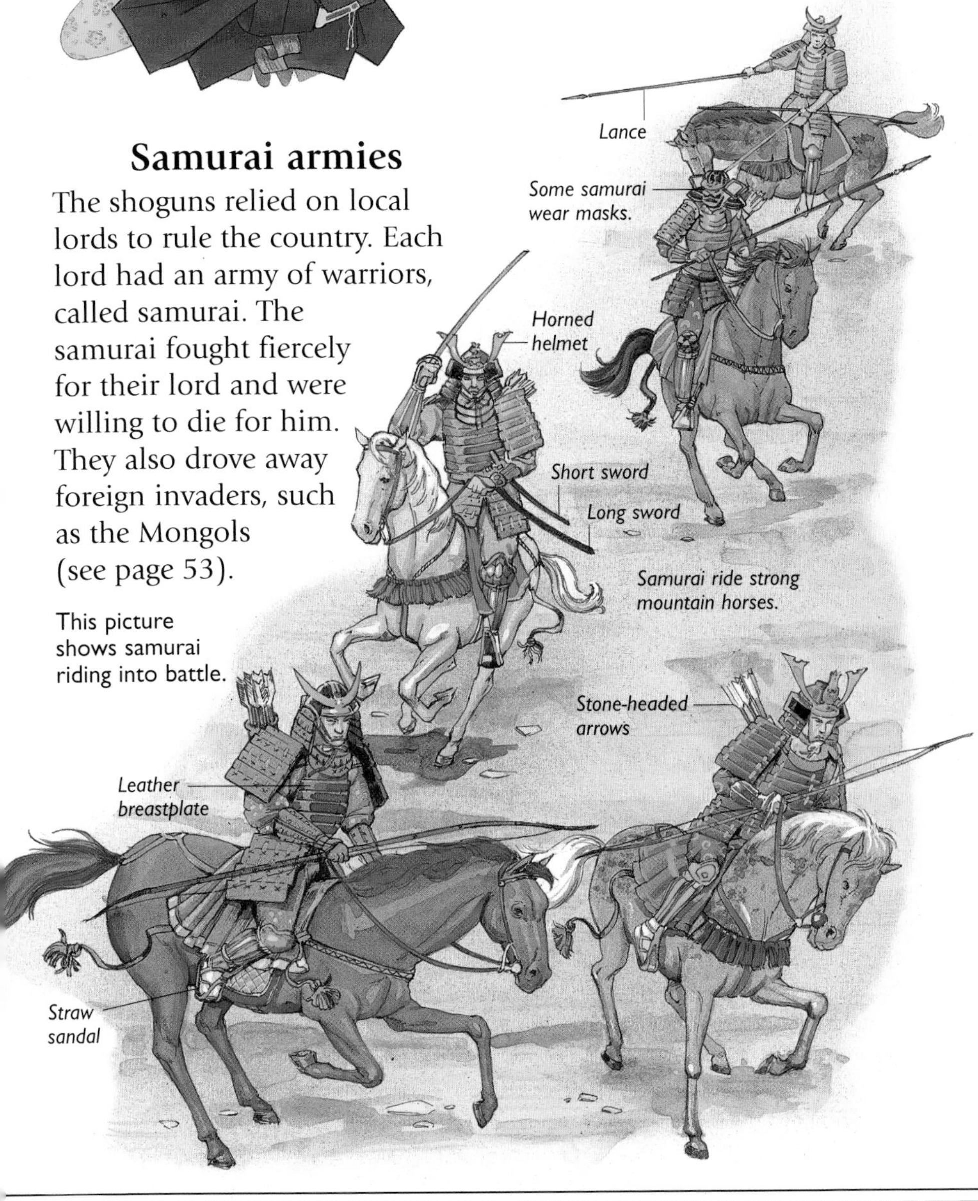

Lance

Some samurai wear masks.

Horned helmet

Short sword

Long sword

Samurai ride strong mountain horses.

Stone-headed arrows

Leather breastplate

Straw sandal

Important dates

500	The Yamato emperors control most of Japan.
710	Nara becomes the capital of Japan.
794	Heian becomes the capital of Japan.
858-1160	The Fujiwaras control Japan.
1192	Minamato Yoritomo becomes the first shogun.
1274-1281	The Mongols try to invade Japan.

THE FAR EAST

Explorers and Sailors

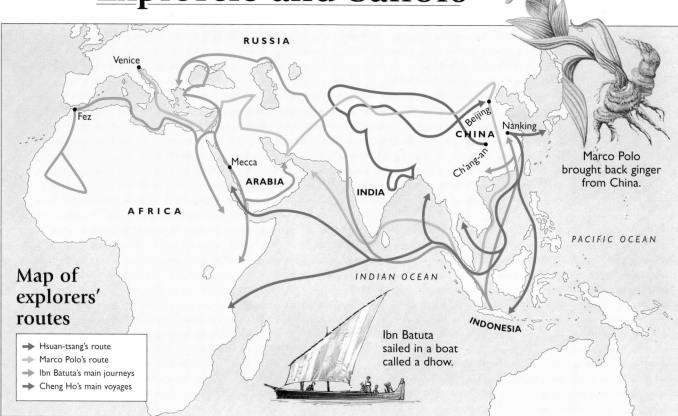

RUSSIA

Venice

Fez

Mecca

ARABIA

AFRICA

Beijing

Nanking

CHINA

Ch'ang-an

INDIA

INDIAN OCEAN

PACIFIC OCEAN

INDONESIA

Marco Polo brought back ginger from China.

Ibn Batuta sailed in a boat called a dhow.

Map of explorers' routes

➤ Hsuan-tsang's route
➤ Marco Polo's route
➤ Ibn Batuta's main journeys
➤ Cheng Ho's main voyages

Travel in the Middle Ages was very difficult and dangerous, but a few brave explorers set out on amazing jouneys. Although traders had reached Africa, India and China, these countries were almost completely unexplored.

Ibn Batuta's dream

Ibn Batuta was a wealthy Muslim from Fez in North Africa. When he was 21, he went on a pilgrimage (religious journey) to Mecca, in Arabia. On the way, he dreamed that a huge bird was carrying him over the Muslim world and beyond. This dream inspired him to spend his life exploring.

Ibn Batuta's dream

A lifetime of travel

An Indian sultan welcoming Ibn Batuta

Ibn Batuta's first journey took him to Arabia, southern Russia and India. Then, he sailed to China. On his second great expedition, he explored parts of Africa. Ibn Batuta covered over 120,000km (75,000 miles) during his 30 years of travel.

Hsuan-tsang goes west

In the 7th century, a Buddhist monk called Hsuan-tsang made the long and dangerous journey from Ch'ang-an in China to northern India. He spent 16 years visiting Indian monasteries and temples. Then, he returned to China with hundreds of manuscripts and statues.

Hsuan-tsang

Marco Polo goes east

Marco Polo left Venice for China when he was 17. He journeyed overland for three and a half years with his father and uncle. In Beijing, the Polos were welcomed by the Mongol emperor, Kublai Khan (see page 71). Marco Polo stayed in China for 17 years, before sailing back to Venice. He told many stories about the sights he had seen and the legends he had heard.

Marco Polo told a story about a man-monster with a single foot.

Cheng Ho's voyages

A Chinese explorer named Cheng Ho went on seven great voyages to Indonesia, Arabia and Africa. He sailed with over 300 ships (called junks), and brought back amazing treasures, such as gold, ivory and wild animals.

This picture shows Cheng Ho returning to China from Africa.

The Chinese emperor waits to welcome Cheng Ho.

Merchants, priests and translators all went on the voyage.

Cheng Ho

Important dates

c.628-645 Hsuan-tsang's travels
1271-1295 Marco Polo's travels
c.1325-1355 Ibn Batuta's travels
1405-1433 Cheng Ho's voyages

THE WORLD

1100   1200   1300   1400   1500

The People of the Pacific

Map of the Pacific

SOUTHEAST ASIA

NORTH PACIFIC OCEAN

POLYNESIA

Breadfruit

Coconut

Sweet potato

Pacific fruit and vegetables

INDIAN OCEAN

AUSTRALIA

SOUTH PACIFIC OCEAN

EASTER ISLAND

NEW ZEALAND

Around 6,000 years ago, settlers from Southeast Asia began arriving in the islands of the Pacific Ocean. They were skilled sailors who studied the winds, stars and ocean currents to help them find their way around. Very slowly, the settlers spread out. By around 400, they had reached as far east as Easter Island.

Island life

Most of the Pacific islanders lived in small tribes ruled by powerful chiefs. They went fishing, gathered fruit, grew vegetables, and kept pigs, dogs and chickens. The islanders prayed to many gods and offered them sacrifices.

This picture shows a Pacific island village.

Coconut palm

These people are setting out to find new land.

Settlers' ship

Wall made from the trunks of coconut palms

Roof made from coconut palm leaves

Canoe

Visitors from other islands trade shells and feathers.

People use leaves as plates.

Women weaving baskets

This man is trying to spear a fish.

Men carving a statue

Big heads

Carved heads on Easter Island

The people of Easter Island carved over 600 huge stone heads and stood them on platforms all around the coast. These statues were probably meant to represent powerful chiefs. Some of them are over 12m (40ft) tall.

Maori settlers

Around 750, a tribe called the Maoris set sail from the islands of Polynesia and reached New Zealand. At first, they survived by fishing, gathering fruit, and hunting large birds. Later, they grew vegetables. By 1500, the Maoris had become very warlike.

Maori chief

Spirits and taboos

The Maoris prayed to the spirits of their dead ancestors. They also believed that certain people and places were sacred. These sacred people and places were called "tapu", or taboo.

Good luck charm showing an ancestor

The first Australians

The Aboriginal people arrived in northern Australia around 40,000 years ago. They walked most of the way from Southeast Asia on land that is now under the sea. Slowly, they spread out all over Australia. The Aboriginals lived by gathering plants and hunting animals. Hunters used boomerangs to help them catch their prey.

Aboriginal hunters

Boomerang

Dream time spirits

Aboriginals believe that they were created by spirits who lived in a time called the dream time. Some of the spirits were humans, and some were animals and plants.

Painting of the Rainbow Serpent giving birth to the Aboriginal people

Banana plant

This man is planting sweet potatoes.

Tower built for a god

These people are bringing offerings to one of their gods.

Important dates

c.400 Settlers reach Easter Island.

c.750 The Maoris reach New Zealand.

c.1000-1600 The Easter Islanders build huge stone heads.

AUSTRALASIA

Native North Americans

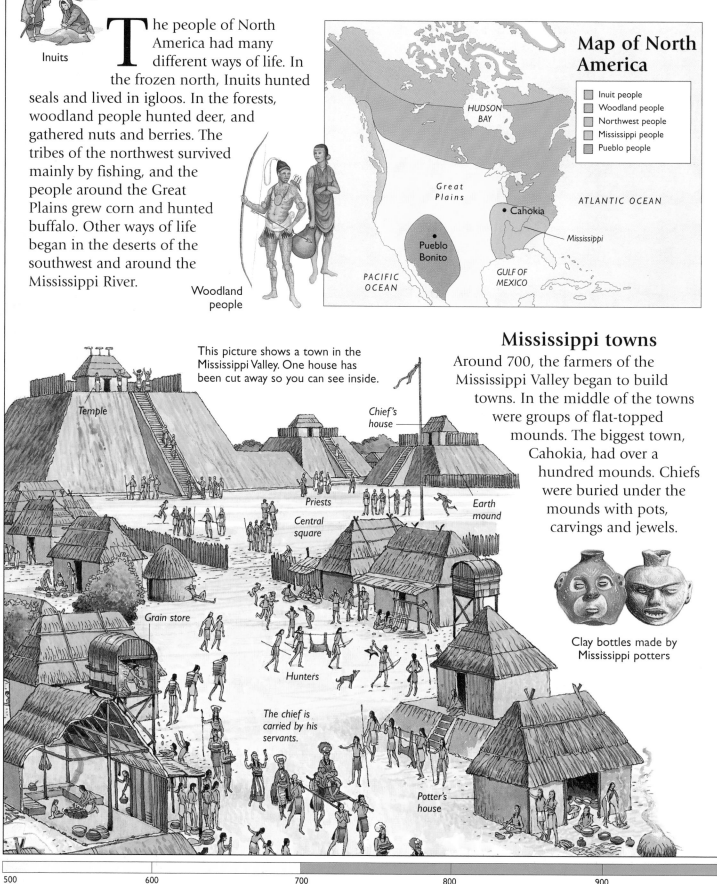

Inuits

The people of North America had many different ways of life. In the frozen north, Inuits hunted seals and lived in igloos. In the forests, woodland people hunted deer, and gathered nuts and berries. The tribes of the northwest survived mainly by fishing, and the people around the Great Plains grew corn and hunted buffalo. Other ways of life began in the deserts of the southwest and around the Mississippi River.

Woodland people

Map of North America

HUDSON BAY

| Inuit people |
| Woodland people |
| Northwest people |
| Mississippi people |
| Pueblo people |

Great Plains

ATLANTIC OCEAN

• Cahokia

Mississippi

Pueblo Bonito

PACIFIC OCEAN

GULF OF MEXICO

This picture shows a town in the Mississippi Valley. One house has been cut away so you can see inside.

Temple

Chief's house

Priests

Central square

Earth mound

Grain store

Hunters

The chief is carried by his servants.

Potter's house

Mississippi towns

Around 700, the farmers of the Mississippi Valley began to build towns. In the middle of the towns were groups of flat-topped mounds. The biggest town, Cahokia, had over a hundred mounds. Chiefs were buried under the mounds with pots, carvings and jewels.

Clay bottles made by Mississippi potters

THE AMERICAS

| 500 | 600 | 700 | 800 | 900 |

Pueblo people

Around 750, some desert tribes in the southwest began to build villages with rooms stacked one above the other. Villages built like this were called pueblos, and the people who lived in them became known as the Pueblos.

In this picture of a pueblo, one house has been cut away to show what is happening inside.

This woman is repairing a wall.

People use ladders to reach their roofs.

The walls are made from dried mud, called adobe.

Weavers make cotton clothes and rugs.

Dried meat

Women grind corn.

Farmers grow corn, beans and cotton.

Clay pots are baked in ovens called kilns.

Potters make and decorate pots.

During the day, people work and eat on the roofs of their houses.

Trading towns

Towns grew up in places where the Pueblo people met to trade with each other and with people from other tribes.

Kiva (sunken room)

Pueblo Bonito

The town of Pueblo Bonito was built inside a deep valley and surrounded by a vast network of roads. It housed around 1200 people in 800 rooms. In the middle of the town were several sunken rooms, called kivas. These rooms were used for religious ceremonies and meetings.

Pueblo crafts

Carvers made ornaments from polished stone, weavers made clothes from brightly dyed cotton, and potters made jugs and pots that were covered with bold patterns.

Painted figure from a Pueblo pot

Pueblo jug

Pierced pots

Special pots were placed in the graves of Pueblo chiefs. The pots were pierced to release the spirits of their painted figures.

Burial pot

Important dates

c.700 The Mississippi people begin to build towns.

c.750 The Pueblo people begin to build villages.

c.1300 The Pueblo people abandon their towns and villages.

c.1500 The Mississippi people abandon their towns.

| 1100 | 1200 | 1300 | 1400 | 1500 |

The Aztec Empire

Priest's knife

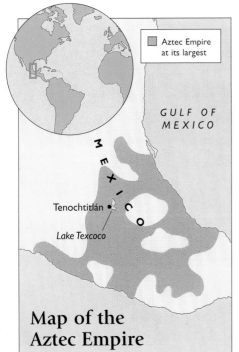

Aztec Empire at its largest

GULF OF MEXICO

MEXICO

Tenochtitlán •

Lake Texcoco

Map of the Aztec Empire

This picture shows part of the city of Tenochtitlán.

The Aztecs were wandering, warlike people who arrived in central Mexico around 1300. They settled on an island in Lake Texcoco and started to build the village of Tenochtitlán. Over the next 200 years, Tenochtitlán grew into a great city and the Aztecs built up an empire around it.

The city on a lake

Tenochtitlán spread over a group of islands at the edge of Lake Texcoco. In the middle of the city was a beautiful square, filled with temples where priests held ceremonies.

Sacrifices to the sun

The Aztecs believed that their sun god, Huitzilopochtli, might die unless they kept him strong. To keep him alive, they fed him human hearts. Priests cut out their victims' hearts, then hurled the bodies down the temple steps.

Aztec priests making human sacrifices

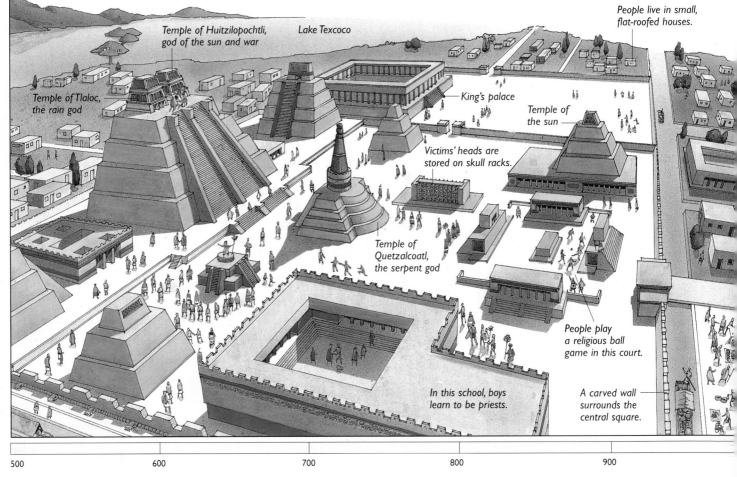

Temple of Huitzilopochtli, god of the sun and war

Lake Texcoco

People live in small, flat-roofed houses.

Temple of Tlaloc, the rain god

King's palace

Temple of the sun

Victims' heads are stored on skull racks.

Temple of Quetzalcoatl, the serpent god

People play a religious ball game in this court.

In this school, boys learn to be priests.

A carved wall surrounds the central square.

The Aztec year

It was important for the Aztecs to know when to hold their festivals. They divided the 365 days of the year into 18 months of 20 days each. The remaining 5 days were believed to be unlucky.

The outer rings of this calendar stone show the days of the year.

The end of the Empire

In 1519, the Spanish soldier Hernando Cortés arrived in Mexico determined to conquer the Aztecs. The Aztecs were terrified by the Spanish guns and horses. Some thought that Quetzalcoatl, the serpent god, had come back to earth.

Mask of Quetzalcoatl

At first, Cortés did not attack the Aztecs, but in 1521 he invaded Tenochtitlán and conquered its people. After this defeat, many Aztecs died from European diseases and their way of life soon disappeared.

The defeat of the Aztecs

Aztec wars

The Aztec army fought constant wars against surrounding tribes. They forced the defeated tribes to give them food and treasure, and took thousands of prisoners to be sacrificed to their gods.

Aztec eagle knight

Floating fields

Farmers filled huge baskets with earth and floated them on lakes. In these floating fields, they grew corn, beans and chili peppers.

An Aztec god protecting a corn plant

Bird attacking the corn

Corn plant

God of planting and spring

Spanish troops arrive on horseback.

Spanish soldiers fire guns at the Aztecs.

Canoe

Bridges link plots of land.

Raised roads join the city to the mainland.

Merchants trade goods in the market.

Crafts

Many Aztecs worked as potters, weavers and carpenters. Sculptors carved huge statues, and craftworkers made beautiful objects from gold and feathers.

Gold pendant

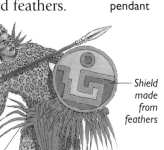

Feathered costume

Shield made from feathers

Aztec warrior

Important dates

c.1300 The Aztecs arrive in the Valley of Mexico.

c.1325 The Aztecs start to build Tenochtitlán.

1420s The Aztecs begin to conquer the surrounding tribes.

c.1500 The Aztecs control the Valley of Mexico.

1521 Cortés conquers the Aztecs.

THE AMERICAS

The Maya and the Toltecs

The Maya people lived in small kingdoms in the rainforests and plains of Central America. They were ruled by powerful kings who were also priests and warriors.

A Mayan king with his servant

Gods and kings

The Maya prayed to many gods and gave them gifts of human blood. They also believed that their kings had godlike powers. Mayan kings were buried under temples and people prayed to them as if they were gods.

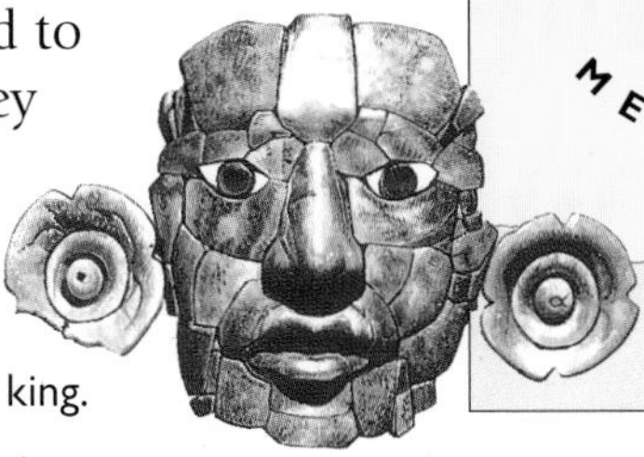

This jade mask was found in the tomb of a Mayan king.

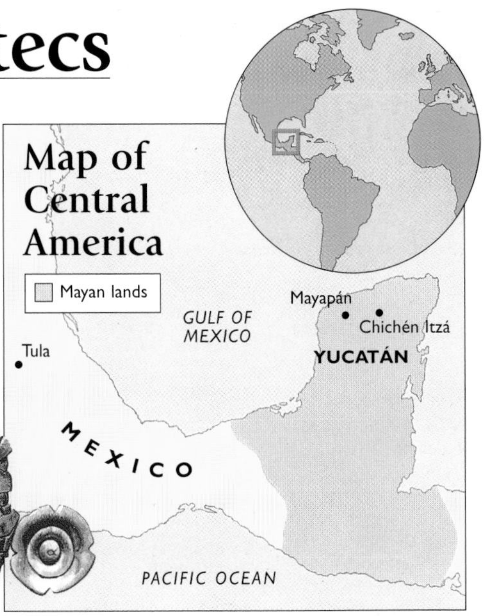

Map of Central America

☐ Mayan lands

GULF OF MEXICO

Tula

Mayapán

Chichén Itzá

YUCATÁN

MEXICO

PACIFIC OCEAN

Cities of stone

Each Mayan kingdom had a splendid capital city built from stone. The king lived in the city with his nobles, warriors and priests. Farmers from the country brought food to the city and came to watch the spectacular ceremonies that were held there.

This picture shows a ceremony in a Mayan city.

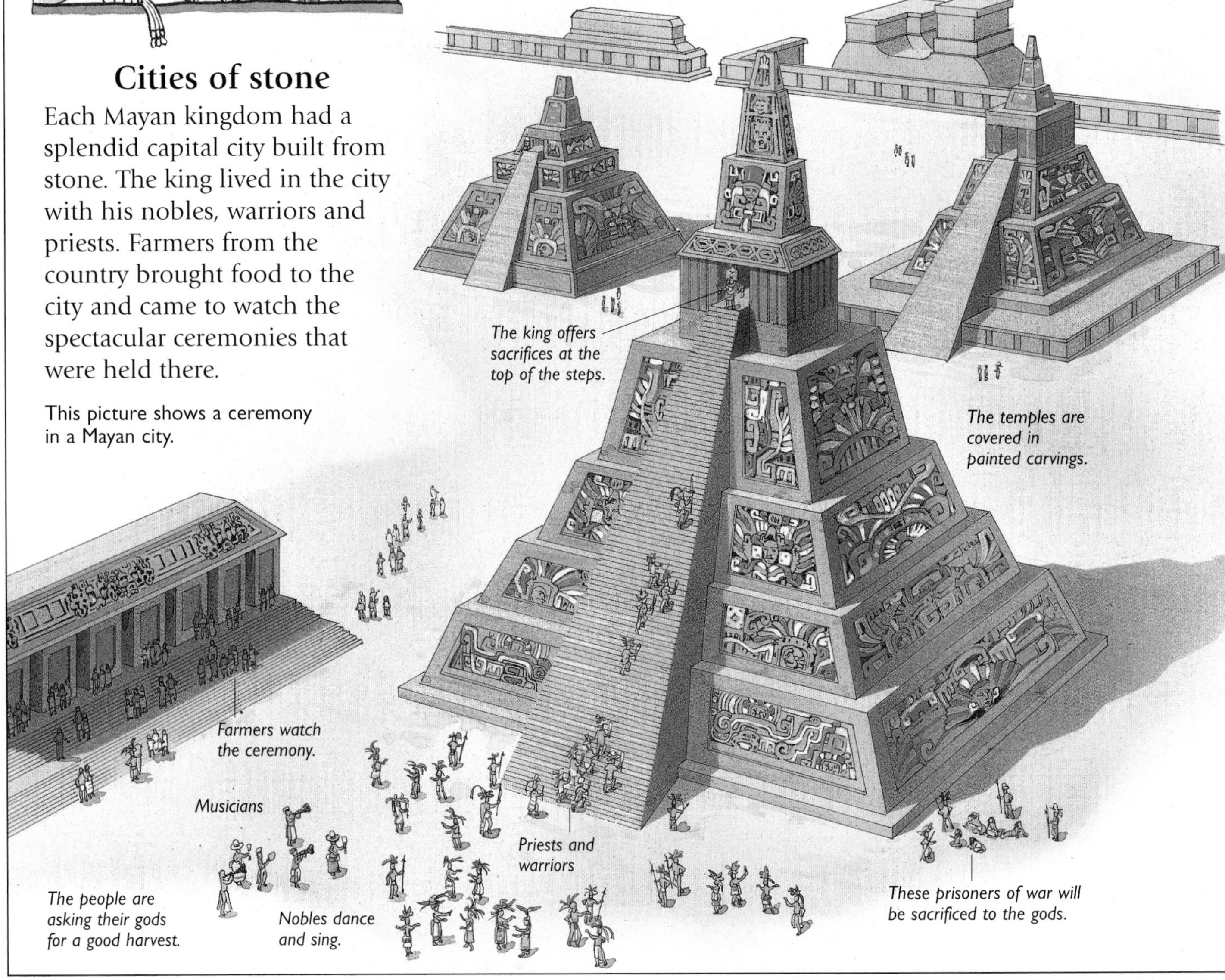

The king offers sacrifices at the top of the steps.

The temples are covered in painted carvings.

Farmers watch the ceremony.

Musicians

Priests and warriors

The people are asking their gods for a good harvest.

Nobles dance and sing.

These prisoners of war will be sacrificed to the gods.

Game of life and death

Young warriors played a fast-moving ball game which was meant to symbolize the battle between life and death. At the end of the game, some players were put to death.

This picture shows a ball game.

Helmet

Players hit a rubber ball with their arms, knees and hips.

Padded belt

Arm guard

Knee guard

Counting the days

Astronomer-priests studied the stars and invented two kinds of calendars. One was a very accurate 365-day calendar. The other was a religious guide which helped the priests to predict the future. They wrote out their calendars using special signs for words and numbers.

Part of a Mayan calendar

Dots, dashes and curved lines show dates.

Carved Toltec warrior

The rise of the Toltecs

Around 850, most of the Maya people moved north into an area known as the Yucatán. Meanwhile, in Mexico, the Toltecs were becoming powerful. The Toltecs controlled Mexico from their capital at Tula. They were warriors, traders and craftworkers.

The city of Chichén Itzá

In the 1100s, invading tribes drove the Toltecs out of Mexico and into the Yucatán. Many Toltecs settled in the Mayan city of Chichén Itzá. The city's Temple of the Warriors was probably built by the Maya and Toltec people working together.

Statue from the Temple of the Warriors

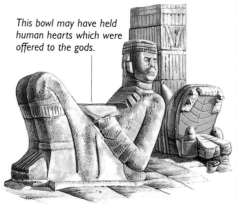

This bowl may have held human hearts which were offered to the gods.

The end of Chichén Itzá

Around 1160, fierce tribes from the north began invading Chichén Itzá. The Toltecs were scattered, and the Maya moved to new cities, such as Mayapán. By 1500, however, the Mayan kingdoms had shrunk to just a few small towns.

Important dates

c.600	The Maya are at their most successful.
c.850	The Maya abandon their cities in the south.
c.900-1000	The Toltecs are powerful in Mexico.
c.1100	The Toltecs arrive in Chichén Itzá.
c.1160	Chichén Itzá is invaded and the Toltecs are scattered.
c.1500	The Maya live in just a few small towns.

Empires of the Andes

The strip of land between the Andes Mountains and the Pacific Ocean was home to several tribes, but one of the most powerful groups was the Chimú. Around 1100, the Chimú people began to conquer other tribes and started building up an empire.

Gold knife showing a Chimú noble

The city of Chan Chan

Part of the city of Chan Chan

By 1200, the Chimú ruler and his nobles controlled a large empire from their capital city at Chan Chan. Potters, weavers and goldsmiths all worked in the city, and farmers brought in food from the surrounding countryside.

— Fish design

Chimú pottery jar

Chimú painting of a man with a serpent

The rise of the Incas

The Incas lived in a small mountain kingdom around the city of Cuzco, but in 1438 their ruler, Pachacuti, set out to win more land. The Incas defeated the Chimú and won large areas of land in the south, creating an empire that stretched along most of the Pacific coast.

Inca warriors

— Mace *Sling*

Painted shield

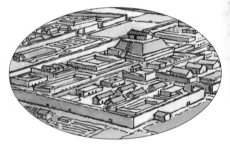

— Leg band made from feathers

Keeping count

The Inca Empire was very well organized and everyone had some kind of work to do. People were fed when food was short, and cared for when they were sick. To make sure the Empire ran smoothly, officials kept records on knotted cords, called quipus.

Quipus

Map of the Chimú and Inca Empires

—	Border of the Chimú Empire
▨	Inca Empire at its largest

Chan Chan

Machu Picchu

Cuzco

SOUTH AMERICA

PACIFIC OCEAN

Andes Mountains

Cities of stone

Even though they had no wheeled vehicles or metal tools, the Incas built amazing cities from stone. The cities had temples, observatories and palaces, as well as ordinary homes.

The mountain city of Machu Picchu

500   600   700   800   900

On the road

A network of roads linked all the parts of the Inca Empire. These roads were used by farmers, traders, messengers and soldiers. The emperor made frequent journeys through his lands to make sure that all his people stayed loyal to him.

This picture shows an Inca emperor on a journey through his empire.

Farmers have built terraces so they can grow crops on the mountainside.

Bridge made from reeds

Storehouse for food

Traders take food to market.

Soldiers march to war.

People can stay overnight in these rest houses.

Farmers grow peppers, chilies, corn and potatoes.

A new messenger will take the bag to the next rest house.

A messenger hands over a bag containing quipus.

The emperor is carried on a throne.

Llamas carry heavy loads.

Royal guard

Young girls sing and dance.

Priest

Musicians play for the emperor.

The end of the Incas

In 1532, a band of Spanish soldiers, called conquistadors, attacked the Incas. Led by Francisco Pizarro, they captured and killed the Inca emperor. This was a great blow to the Incas, and within a few years the Empire collapsed.

Important dates

c.1100	The Chimú start to build their Empire.
c.1300	The Incas settle around Cuzco.
1438-1471	Pachacuti is Emperor of the Incas.
1438-1525	The Inca Empire grows.
1476	The Incas conquer the Chimú Empire.
1532	Spanish conquistadors attack the Incas.
c.1540	The Inca Empire ends.

THE AMERICAS

1100   1200   1300   1400   1500

Artists of Italy

Around 1350, artists and thinkers in northern Italy became very interested in the art, architecture and learning of ancient Greece and Rome. They began to try out new ideas based on what they had learned. This movement is known as the Renaissance, which means "rebirth".

Patrons

Princes, popes and merchants paid money to artists, architects and writers and encouraged them to create works of art. Rich people who supported artists were known as patrons.

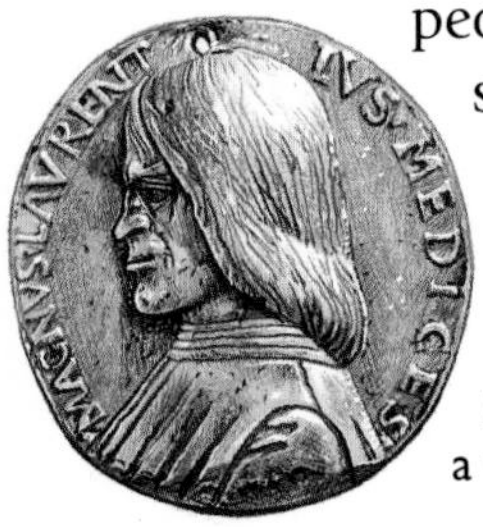
MAGNUS LAURENTIUS MEDICES

Medal showing Lorenzo de' Medici, a famous patron

Florence and the Medicis

The most powerful patrons of the Renaissance were the Medicis, a family of bankers from Florence. The Medicis encouraged artists and scholars to work in their city, and many new ideas were first tried out in Florence.

This picture shows the main square in Florence.

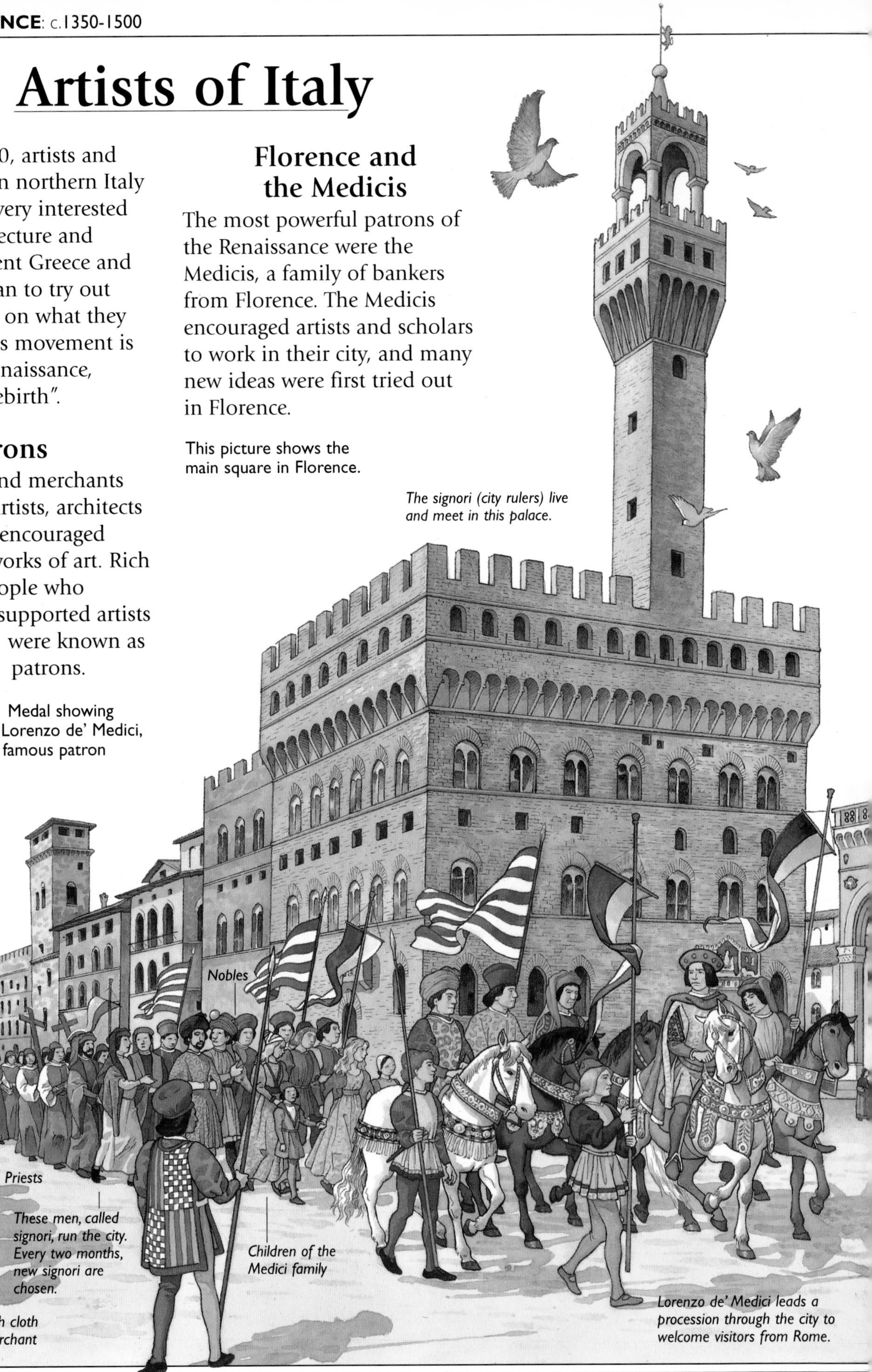
The signori (city rulers) live and meet in this palace.
Nobles
Priests
These men, called signori, run the city. Every two months, new signori are chosen.
Children of the Medici family
Lorenzo de' Medici leads a procession through the city to welcome visitors from Rome.
Beggar
Rich cloth merchant

500 600 700 800 900

Architects

Architects designed buildings with pillars, rounded arches and domes. This style of building was created by the Greeks and Romans and is called classical architecture.

Florence Cathedral

One of the first examples of the new classical style was the dome of Florence Cathedral, designed by the architect Brunelleschi.

This covered area is called a loggia. People hold meetings here.

Scholars discussing new ideas

An architect showing some plans to his patron

Lawyers

An artist sketching a building

Painters

Primavera, by the painter Sandro Botticelli, shows a legend about the coming of Spring.

Inspired by Greek and Roman art, painters tried to make their pictures look as lifelike as possible. They discovered that things in the distance look smaller than things that are close up. They used this effect, called perspective, to give their pictures a feeling of depth.

Before the Renaissance, artists in Europe painted mainly religious pictures, but by 1400 the artists of Italy had become much more adventurous. As well as religious pictures, they painted portraits, landscapes, recent events, and scenes from Greek and Roman legends.

Sculptors

Sculptors copied Greek and Roman statues and used real people as models for their work. They even examined dead bodies to find out how bones and muscles worked. The statues of the Renaissance looked lifelike, strong and graceful.

Statue of David, a famous character in the Bible, by the sculptor and painter Michelangelo

EUROPE

| 1100 | 1200 | 1300 | 1400 | 1500 |

Ideas and Inventions

By the 1400s, many people were studying the works of the ancient Greeks and Romans. These works made them realize how much human beings could achieve, and started a new belief in human ability. This belief, called humanism, spread all over Europe, as artists, writers and scientists tried out new ideas.

Scientists and inventors

During the Renaissance, people started to ask new questions about the world. They carried out scientific experiments and studied plants, animals and humans. Inventors worked on new ideas for clocks, weapons, telescopes, water pumps and other machines.

This picture is based on a design for a flying machine by Leonardo da Vinci.

The flying machine would have been too heavy to get off the ground.

Frame made from beech wood

Wings made from heavy silk

Rope used for steering

These pedals make the wings flap up and down.

Education

Before the Renaissance, only priests were educated, but during the 1400s this began to change. Boys from wealthy families went to school, and rich girls were taught at home by tutors. Pupils studied the writings of the Greeks and Romans, as well as music, art and foreign languages.

Boys at school

Leonardo da Vinci

Leonardo da Vinci was a perfect example of a well-educated Renaissance man. He was an artist, an inventor, an architect and a musician. He made detailed drawings of animals and people, and created designs for amazing machines.

Leonardo da Vinci

Drawings of the human body by Leonardo da Vinci

Leonardo cut up human bodies, so that he could draw and study them.

500   600   700

Alchemists

Many people in Renaissance Europe worked as alchemists. They tried to find a way to turn ordinary metal into gold, and some even thought that they could create a magic potion that would give people eternal life. Alchemists learned how to make chemicals and invented lots of scientific equipment.

An alchemist's laboratory

Flasks of boiling chemicals

This man is using scales to weigh powder.

The alchemist follows instructions in a manuscript.

Hourglass used for timing experiments

This boy is grinding powder with a pestle and mortar.

The birth of printing

In the 1450s, a German named Johann Gutenberg invented a machine called a printing press, which printed books a page at a time. Until then, all books in Europe had been copied by hand.

Wooden press

Paper

Metal letters arranged in a block and covered with ink

A printing press

Writers and thinkers

Poets began to write about human feelings, and thinkers discussed how countries should be run. An Italian called Niccolò Machiavelli wrote a book called "The Prince", which said that a ruler should always do what was best for his kingdom, even if it meant being cruel and ruthless.

Niccolò Machiavelli

Page from an early printed book

Soon, printing presses were set up all over Europe. Books were produced quickly and cheaply, and this helped to spread the new ideas of Renaissance thinkers and scientists.

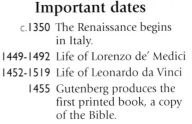

Important dates

c.1350   The Renaissance begins in Italy.

1449-1492   Life of Lorenzo de' Medici

1452-1519   Life of Leonardo da Vinci

1455   Gutenberg produces the first printed book, a copy of the Bible.

1469-1527   Life of Niccolò Machiavelli

EUROPE

1100	1200	1300	1400	1500

Voyages of Discovery

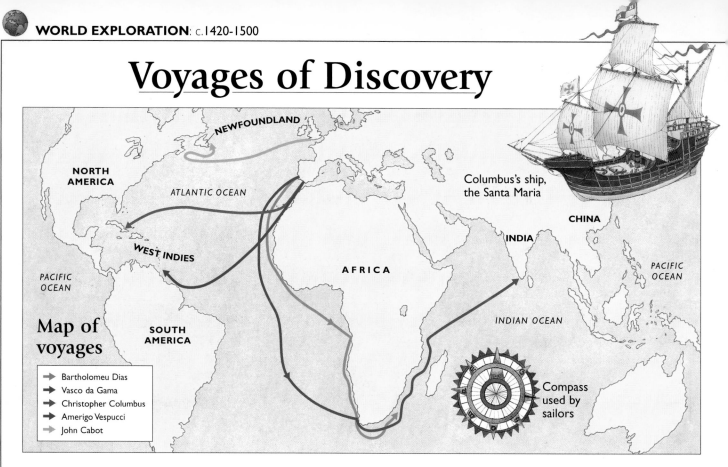

NEWFOUNDLAND

NORTH AMERICA

ATLANTIC OCEAN

Columbus's ship, the Santa Maria

CHINA

INDIA

WEST INDIES

PACIFIC OCEAN

AFRICA

PACIFIC OCEAN

INDIAN OCEAN

Map of voyages

- ➡ Bartholomeu Dias
- ➡ Vasco da Gama
- ➡ Christopher Columbus
- ➡ Amerigo Vespucci
- ➡ John Cabot

SOUTH AMERICA

Compass used by sailors

Large areas of the world were completely unknown to the people of medieval Europe. Explorers and traders had reached North Africa, India and China, but no one had any idea that America existed.

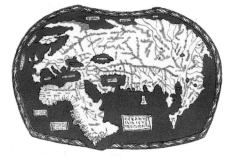

This map, made in 1489, shows how people saw the world at that time.

Finding a way east

By the 1450s, traders in Europe were desperate to find a way to the East by sea. Silks and spices from India and China were in great demand, but they had to be carried overland on long and dangerous journeys.

Henry the Navigator

Prince Henry of Portugal, known as Henry the Navigator, was convinced that ships could reach India by sailing south around Africa.

Henry the Navigator

He persuaded Portuguese explorers to sail south, even though they believed that the southern seas were boiling hot and filled with monsters. Henry paid for nearly 20 expeditions along the west coast of Africa.

Early artist's view of a sea monster

Sailing around Africa

In 1487, a storm blew the ship of a Portuguese explorer, Bartholomeu Dias, around the southern tip of Africa.

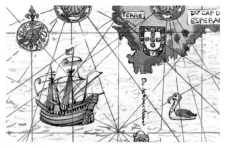

Part of a map showing a ship sailing around southern Africa

After this, other ships sailed around Africa, and in 1498 Vasco da Gama reached India by this route.

Christopher Columbus

Most people in the Middle Ages thought that the world was flat, but a few believed it was round. An Italian captain, named Christopher Columbus, was sure that he could reach China by heading west and sailing all the way around the world. He persuaded the King and Queen of Spain to pay for his voyage.

Columbus's ships wait in the port.

The Santa Maria

This picture shows Columbus leaving Spain.

The Niña

The Pinta

Sailors check their food supplies for the voyage.

Columbus

King Ferdinand of Spain

Queen Isabella

Courtiers

Columbus finds land

After five weeks, Columbus arrived in the West Indies, a group of islands close to Central America. Columbus thought that he had reached the East, but people soon realized that he had discovered an exciting new land. They called this land the "New World".

Columbus arriving in the West Indies

Amerigo Vespucci

In 1499, another Italian, Amerigo Vespucci, reached the mainland of America. Vespucci sailed down the coast of South America as far as the Amazon River. America was named after him in 1507.

Amerigo Vespucci

John Cabot

In 1497, an expedition set out from England, led by an Italian captain called John Cabot. Cabot crossed the Atlantic Ocean in search of India, but instead he reached Newfoundland, off the coast of North America.

Important dates

c.1420-1460 Henry the Navigator encourages Portuguese expeditions.

1487 Bartholomeu Dias sails around Africa.

1492 Christopher Columbus discovers the West Indies.

1497 John Cabot reaches Newfoundland.

1498 Vasco da Gama sails to India.

1499 Amerigo Vespucci reaches South America.

The Spanish flag

Some Native Americans give the sailors presents.

Columbus

The sailors carry weapons.

Sailors planting a cross

THE WORLD

1100   1200   1300   1400   1500

World Time Chart

This chart shows what was happening at the same time in different parts of the world.

DATE	THE AMERICAS	EUROPE	AFRICA
Before 500		c.450 The Angles, Saxons and Jutes begin to rule Britain.	429 The Vandals invade North Africa.
500	c.600 The Maya are at their most successful. Mayan mask	481-511 Clovis creates the kingdom of the Franks. 507 The Visigoths invade Spain. 527-565 Justinian rules the Byzantine Empire. Coin showing Justinian	533 The Byzantines conquer North Africa. 697 The Arabs conquer North Africa.
700	c.700 The Mississippi people start to build towns. c.850 Many Mayan towns are abandoned.	711 The Moors invade Spain. c.790 The Vikings begin raiding Europe. 800-814 Charlemagne rules his Empire. c.862 Rurik creates a kingdom in Russia.	c.700 The kingdom of Ghana is at its most successful.
900	c.900 The Pueblo people start to build towns. c.900-1200 The Toltecs are powerful. c.1000 Leif Ericson reaches North America.	962-973 Otto I is the first Holy Roman Emperor. Emperor Otto's crown 1037-1492 The Christians win back Spain from the Moors. 1054 The Church in eastern Europe splits from the Church in western Europe. 1066 The Normans conquer England.	969-1171 The Fatimids rule Egypt. c.1000 The kingdoms of Benin and Ife are created.
1100	c.1100 The Chimú start to build their Empire.	c.1100 The Viking raids end. 1215 King John of England signs Magna Carta. King John c.1250-1480 The Mongols rule southern Russia.	c.1200 The kingdom of Mali is created. 1250-1517 The Mamelukes rule Egypt.
1300	c.1300 The Pueblo people abandon their towns. c.1345 The Aztecs start to build their Empire. Aztec warrior 1438 The Incas start to build their Empire.	c.1300 The city of Moscow starts to beome powerful. 1337-1453 The French and the English fight the Hundred Years' War. 1347-1353 The Black Death spreads through Europe. c.1350 The Renaissance begins in Italy. 1378-1417 Rival popes rule in Avignon and Rome. Florence Cathedral	c.1350 The city of Great Zimbabwe is at its largest.
1450	1492 Columbus discovers the West Indies.	1453 The Ottoman Turks capture Constantinople and the Byzantine Empire collapses.	c.1450 The Portuguese start trading in West Africa.

A S I A			AUSTRALASIA
THE MIDDLE EAST	SOUTH ASIA	THE FAR EAST	
			c.400 Settlers reach Easter Island.
c.570-632 The life of Mohammed. 632 Arab caliphs (rulers) start to build the Islamic Empire.		Sui Emperor's boat 581 The Sui dynasty begins in China. 618 The Tang dynasty begins in China.	
750 The Abbasid Caliphs start to rule the Islamic Empire from Baghdad.	711 The Arabs invade northern India. 886 The Chola kingdom is created in southern India.	802 The Khmer kingdom is created in Cambodia. 858 The Fujiwara family take control in Japan. 868 The earliest printed book is produced in China.	c.750 The Maoris reach New Zealand. Maori good luck charm
1055 The Seljuk Turks capture Baghdad and control the Islamic Empire. 1071 The Seljuk Turks beat the Byzantines at the Battle of Manzikert. 1096 The Crusades begin. 1099 The Crusaders capture parts of Palestine.		960 The Sung dynasty begins in China. Painting by a Sung artist	c.1000 The Easter Islanders start to build stone heads.
1258 The Mongols capture Baghdad. 1290 Osman I starts to build the Ottoman Empire. Osman I 1291 The Crusades end.	1206 The Sultans of Delhi start to rule northern India.	1192 Shoguns start to take control in Japan. c.1230 The Sukhothai kingdom is created in Thailand. Statue from the Sukhothai kingdom 1206-1226 Genghis Khan builds the Mongol Empire. 1279-1368 The Mongols rule China.	
1360-1405 Tamerlane builds a new Mongol Empire. Tamerlane	1336 The kingdom of Vijayanagar is created in southern India. 1398 Tamerlane invades northern India.	1368 The Ming dynasty begins in China.	

93

Word List

This list explains some of the more difficult words that are used in the book.

archbishop An important Christian priest, in charge of the Church over a large area.

barbarian A member of one of the warlike tribes that came from the lands outside the Roman Empire.

Barbarian brooch

bishop An important Christian priest, who has the rank below an archbishop.

caliph An Arab ruler.

crusade A war fought for a religious reason.

duchy An area of land that is ruled by a powerful nobleman called a duke.

dynasty A series of rulers from the same family.

empire A large group of lands that is ruled by one powerful person.

fortress A group of buildings surrounded by a wall so that they can be easily defended.

guild An organization for craftworkers or traders, which had strict rules for all its members.

Blacksmiths' guild badge

herald A person who announces something and carries messages.

heretic A Christian whose ideas were different from the teachings of the Church.

icon A religious picture, usually painted on a wooden panel.

Russian icon of the Archangel Michael

Islam The religion based on the teachings of Mohammed.

khan A Mongol ruler.

knight A man trained to fight on horseback for his lord.

lance A long pole with a pointed end, used as a weapon.

manuscript A handwritten book or document.

mosaic A picture made from lots of small pieces of stone or glass.

mosque A building where Muslims pray.

Muslim A person who follows the religion of Islam.

observatory A building from which people study the stars.

pagan A person who believes in many gods.

patron A rich person who pays artists, architects or writers to produce works of art.

peasant A person in the Middle Ages who worked on the land.

pilgrimage A journey to a holy place.

plague A disease which spreads fast and usually kills people.

pueblo A village or town built by the Pueblo people in the southwest of North America.

The town of Pueblo Bonito

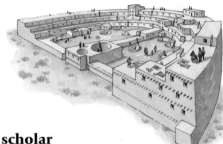

scholar A person who studies, teaches, and writes books.

standard-bearer A soldier who carries his leader's flag into battle.

stocks A heavy wooden frame with holes in it, used for locking up criminals.

sultan A ruler of the Ottoman Empire or of other Muslim lands.

tsar A Russian emperor.

yurt A circular tent made from felt or animal skins, used in central Asia.

Index

Pages where you can find out most about a subject are shown in **bold** type.

Picture credits: Ancient Art and Architecture/Ronald
Sheridan, 5, 9, 22; Bridgeman Art Library, 51, 87;
e.t. archive, 7; Clive Gifford, 77; © Michael Holford, 61;
National Gallery, London, 41, 48; Robert Harding Picture
Library/Sybil Sassoon, 83.

First published in 1999 by Usborne Publishing Ltd, Usborne House, 83-85 Saffron Hill,
London EC1N 8RT, England. www.usborne.com Copyright © 1999 Usborne Publishing Ltd.

First published in America 1999 UE. The name Usborne and the device 🎈 are Trade Marks of
Usborne Publishing Ltd. All rights reserved. No part of this publication may be reproduced, stored in
a retrieval system, or transmitted in any form or by any means, electronic, mechanical, photocopying,
recording or otherwise, without the prior permission of the publisher. Printed in Dubai.